NOBODY
IS
BROKEN

Published in the UK in 2021 by Incrediball Publishing

Copyright © Lucinda Gordon Lennox 2021

Lucinda Gordon Lennox has asserted her right under
the Copyright, Designs and Patents Act, 1988,
to be identified as the author of this work.

Paperback ISBN 978-1-9196322-0-9
eBook   ISBN 978-1-9196322-1-6

Cover design and typeset by SpiffingCovers.com

NOBODY
IS
BROKEN

WE ALL HAVE SOME TRAUMA · AND TRAUMA CAN BE HEALED ·

LUCINDA GORDON LENNOX

CONTENTS

PREFACE

So much has changed in the time since I thought about writing this book. A global Covid-19 pandemic has been going on for over a year, we are properly realising the dire state of planet earth that we, as humans, have unwittingly caused, and there is a global shift in consciousness occurring. These are times unparalleled in written history.

Relative to the enormity of what is occurring in the world right now, the notion of individual trauma, at first glance, might seem trite. But I think the reverse is true. I truly believe that resolving and healing our unresolved past trauma – of which we all do have at least some – will help us not just to survive this global pandemic and all that it brings, but that it will also help us to navigate the vast changes that are occurring on earth and on other dimensions.

A beautiful side effect of healing our trauma is a reintegrating of the fragmented parts of ourselves back into the whole. At last we can find our centre, and we can be still in the present moment. We are no longer living in a heightened or depressed state, but are able to sit, in peace, hearing the quiet of our minds and the call of our souls. And, on an expanded level, the whole is comprised of us, humans, and of planet earth and the cosmos. To love the planet is to love ourselves, and to love ourselves and the planet is to love the divine. Healing our trauma, individually and collectively, is to my mind a really important piece of the jigsaw. This is the book I wished I had been able to read when I was younger, suffering intensely, believing there was something terribly wrong with me and fully believing that I was permanently damaged. Through trauma work, both personally and professionally, I have learned that not only was I neither wrong nor damaged, but that actually nobody is – nobody. We are all whole beings with some lost and fragmented parts that are waiting to be rediscovered and reintegrated into our conscious being. We are not broken – even if we feel like we are. What is evident, however, is that we are in a trauma epidemic of vast proportions, both individually and as a collective, within which we are all unwittingly hiding a tonne of our hurt.

Nobody is broken. And I really do believe that we can all heal. But the healing journey can be hard work.

I hope that this book will help those to whom taking the first step on the healing journey feels too frightening: for you, I hope this book will help you to realise that none of your past was your fault and that you are not bad, nor broken. And for others, who have already started the healing process, I hope that this book helps you gain clarity around yourself and your past, gaining further perspective on how you can continue moving forward.

INTRODUCTION

What is trauma?

*"Trauma is perhaps the most avoided, ignored,
belittled, denied, misunderstood and untreated
cause of human suffering"*

– Peter Levine

Trauma is not just something that happens to other people –
this is fortunately now an outdated myth. Over the past decades
and over the past twenty years in particular, the research
on trauma has accelerated incredibly fast. What began as
empathic curiosity treating soldiers returning from Vietnam,
has now ballooned into a full-scale operation of research and
treatment for many people, across many continents, suffering
with many ailments. We now understand that trauma is not
confined just to war veterans. We now understand that trauma
is everywhere.

And we all have at least some. We all have at least some
unresolved trauma.

If we think of a really horrific event or experience, we might
agree that said event or experience is "trauma". Many events
and experiences are classed as traumatic; we might all be able
to identify with that.

But trauma is way, way, way more than this. Trauma is the unresolved imprint of any past event, or experience, that is still causing us some distress in our current lives.

"We have learned that trauma is not just an event that took place sometime in the past; it is also the imprint left by that experience on mind, brain and body"
– Bessel van der Kolk

Trauma is actually less about what happened and much, much more about the imprint from whatever happened left on our mind, brain and body. This imprint has caused us continued suffering long after the event or experience has passed. Of course, the event or experience caused the trauma, but the trauma itself is much more about how our system is responding.

None of us can expect to live our life successfully processing everything that happens to us – it is simply not possible in the world in which we live.

We might be carrying trauma from a huge, past event that was horrifying. But we might also be carrying trauma from smaller, seemingly less significant events of the past. Many people carry trauma from both huge things that happened and also the little things that happened.

And many of us carry a lot more of this than we realise.

This book talks mainly about those smaller, seemingly less significant events from the past. There is nothing in this book that I have discovered or invented myself. It is much more a compilation of what other great people have discovered before me. Trauma is a complex topic and I hope I have made it relatively simple to understand.

This book will take you on a journey into understanding trauma – the trauma that exists, unprocessed, in all of us.

I will help you to understand where our trauma has come from, how it has happened, and how and why it has remained hidden for so long. I will talk about how it manifests in signs and symptoms throughout our daily lives. Some of these insights might surprise you – they surprised me, as I gradually learned the enormity of the trauma epidemic that we face.

I will help you to understand how family dynamics can contribute to our emotional wounding, and we will look at the notion of generational trauma. We will talk about shame. We will look at sexual trauma and, in particular, childhood sexual abuse. And we will look in some detail at the complexities of the parent-child relationship that can damage us so easily if not managed adequately by our caregivers.

And we will talk about healing. The case studies throughout the book will demonstrate how healing is possible and the final chapter will look at the notion of healing from our trauma in more detail.

I wrote this book because I want us to understand that we can heal. But it is not a "how-to" on healing trauma. Instead, it is a straightforward perspective on what is likely to be the root of suffering for many of us. I sincerely believe that the first step in healing our trauma is to understand that we have trauma. I believe that, in order to heal, we need to understand how we have come to be traumatised, how it has all happened and how it has remained hidden for so long.

I hope that the case studies will serve as inspiration for you.

Underneath almost all mental ill health is unresolved trauma.

Our unresolved trauma is responsible for an enormous amount of the anxiety and stress that exists within us. For some of us, our signs and symptoms of trauma may overwhelm us; for others, they might be there in the background. But regardless of intensity, these signs and symptoms will be hindering our lives.

However heavy or not our trauma might feel to us, it will be preventing us from living a life of true authenticity and peace.

We all have some trauma. And trauma can be healed.

CHAPTER 1

Developmental Trauma

Trauma comes from the horrific things that happen to us.
It also comes from the loving things that didn't happen for us.

I can't tell you the number of people who state the words "I don't have any trauma". You might be thinking that too. Someone might have an eating disorder, or be struggling with an addiction, or anxiety, or depression, or relationship difficulties, or anger. Or they might be a people-pleaser, or behave narcissistically, or say "yes" when they mean "no", be a perfectionist, not feel worthy or good enough, or carry feelings of shame or fear. Or even just have a sense that something is not quite right, that life could be more, but they don't know why or how. But people adamantly say that they don't have any trauma.

When people say that they don't have trauma, they share the commonly understood definition of trauma – that trauma is something big and horrific that happened in the past. For example, suffering after witnessing war zones, after being physically abused, or suffering after being kidnapped, after being in a car crash, after the death of a loved one, or terrorism, or sexual abuse. And, of course, these events are traumatic indeed, and it's always good to hear when people haven't endured that type of trauma. This type of trauma that they are saying they don't have (and often do not) is called Big T trauma, mainly because it was discovered first, but also because the events we are talking about are big. They are horrible, horrific, and / or terrifying. Technically, and according to the diagnostic manual used by psychiatrists and the medical profession (the *Diagnostic and Statistical Manual of Mental Disorders* – DSM), a Big T trauma is caused by something happening whereby we fear our physical life is in danger.

But there is another type of trauma, and this one most people don't know about. This other type of trauma is what I am going to be predominantly talking about in this book.

This other type of trauma is called Little T trauma. Or developmental trauma. Or relational trauma. Or attachment trauma. It has an awful lot of different names for something that most people don't know about!

Many people know this type of trauma as "Little T" trauma. But I am going to say right now that there is nothing "little" at all about Little T trauma or its impact. We need to change this terminology.

Let's look at what this type of trauma is.

There is ongoing debate in the medical world around the classifications of trauma, post-traumatic stress disorder (PTSD), complex PTSD, discrepancies between the DSM and the *International Classification of Diseases* (ICD), and I'm not going to get into the debates here. If you're interested, you are welcome to look them up. But I will make the point that this developmental / relational / attachment / Little T trauma is also still misunderstood by many in the medical profession.

So that we don't all get thoroughly confused, I am going to refer to this other, lesser-known type of trauma as developmental trauma throughout this book.

Developmental trauma is the type of trauma that I treat with 99% of my clients, regardless of what they have come into therapy for. That's 99% of my clients, regardless of what they have come to therapy for. And yes, I did repeat that sentence. And I will repeat that one more time: 99% of my clients have developmental trauma – they just don't know it.

From the shy housewife looking forward every day to her glass of wine at "wine o'clock", to the successful entrepreneur, the family man or woman who just feels a bit stuck, or the quietly anxious, right through to the binge drinker, the terrified agoraphobic who simply can't leave the house, the heroin addict or alcoholic, or the chronically depressed who just wishes they would die. Whatever their presenting symptoms or difficulties, it is always developmental trauma that needs to be addressed – and sometimes Big T trauma too, of course – in order that that person can start to live life as a fully functional, emotionally whole adult, free from the symptoms or dysfunctional adult behaviours that have brought them to therapy in the first place.

When Clare first started with me, she had heard of trauma, but she said she definitely didn't have any. She told me she hadn't ever been sexually or physically abused, she hadn't been in a terrorist attack, nor witnessed one, nor in war zones, car crashes, no deaths of loved ones, no major accidents or hospital admissions – she really didn't think that she had suffered anything traumatic in her life at all. On the contrary, she would tell me, she had lived a really privileged life with a lovely home, lovely schools, and she described everything as "really normal". Yet, as far back as she could remember, she had had low-level anxiety that she just couldn't shift. On top of this, she found herself married to someone she thought she didn't love, by whom she felt suffocated, with whom she had three children. She felt trapped and sad, with no idea what to do or how to feel better. She wanted to leave her husband but felt so guilty about the idea of splitting up the family that when she entertained the idea she would be consumed by fear and wouldn't be able to think straight. She found herself really looking forward to that glass of wine every evening, often not even able to face her husband without a drink inside her, and she was feeling guilty about that too.

David was referred to me and said he didn't have any trauma. He just had a sense that there was something missing from his life, but he couldn't put his finger on what that might be. He found himself watching porn secretly, despite being happily married, feeling desperately guilty about what he was doing.

Rebecca came because she couldn't stand being in the same room as her sister and always felt walked over and trodden on and had no idea how to stop this happening.

Belinda was referred to me because she continued to explode with anger at her children and didn't know how to stop.

Sarah came to me because her mother was continuing to take over her life, even though she was now 45 years old, and she couldn't stand it anymore. But she didn't know how to stop it, and she felt tremendous guilt around potentially putting in some boundaries with her mother.

Annabelle came because she had a terror of getting on aeroplanes and couldn't understand why, as she had never been in a plane crash – or even a car crash for that matter.

Macy came because she had been trying for so long to manifest her dreams and her life; she had taken courses with many of the great manifesting coaches – Joe Dispenza, Wayne Dyer, Gabby Bernstein, Caroline Myss and others – but she could never get to the bit where you had to "feel" the happiness and gratitude in order to allow the manifesting to happen, and she didn't understand why; instead she felt hopeless and useless and not good enough that she couldn't even do that. On further investigation, we also found that she was a bit of a perfectionist, scared of not doing well enough as a wife and a mother and putting herself under a lot of pressure to "get it right" for her husband and her children.

All of these clients – even though they thought they had no trauma – were suffering with unresolved trauma. Some of them were not even aware that there was another way, a better way, free from the internal struggle, free from their struggle with themselves and with life.

And there are even more people suffering in silence, often not thinking that their struggles are large enough to warrant therapy. But they are not happy, they are not fulfilled. If you are one of these, I hope this book will help you to see that it doesn't need to be this way. There is another way. We can bask in the sunshine of life, and we can feel the full spectrum of feelings without becoming overwhelmed by the difficult ones. We can set boundaries that work for us as an individual without hurting others or letting others down.

No matter how large or small our childhood trauma, we can heal.

All of the clients I have mentioned above have looked at, and worked on, their developmental trauma. Once we had treated it, the symptoms that had brought them to therapy in the first place were massively reduced – for most, the symptoms disappeared entirely. For some it took a few sessions, for others it took more, but they all now have much relief and really enjoy life burden-free, anxiety-free – and largely addiction-free too.

So, what is this developmental trauma, and how do we get it?

Developmental trauma is a result of horrible things that happen to us, *and it is also the result of loving things that don't happen for us*, between the ages of 0-18 – in other words, whilst we are a child.

There is a notion that "trauma happens to other people". This notion is incorrect. We actually all have some trauma, some developmental trauma, and some of us have more of it than others. But we all have some. If we have a niggle that something isn't quite glorious in our lives, then we have some developmental trauma.

Physical, sexual and emotional abuse and neglect aged 0-18

We can look at developmental trauma as a result of physical, sexual and emotional abuse and / or neglect, from the age of 0-18, where the resulting trauma is not classed as a Big T. So, we might not feel like our physical life is in danger, but we still suffer as a result of it.

Actually, developmental trauma can start in the womb, as we'll see from some of my case examples – and even before we were conceived, which we will also get to later in the book.

But first, let's look at those three types of abuse and neglect– physical, sexual and emotional, and really make sure we understand what they mean. Some we may find obvious, others less so.

Physical abuse

Physical abuse is when someone intentionally causes injury or harm to another person by physical contact – hitting, kicking, pinching, punching, grabbing, pushing, or any other physical form of harm. It is, if you like, an attempt to control another person through harmful, physical contact. It can be deeply wounding and scarring, both physically and emotionally. Extreme and frequent cases of this would be classified as Big T trauma, and a child would likely end up in foster care if the abuse were discovered.

But what about when hitting is "normalised" within a family? Those children who were regularly smacked by their mum and dad as "part of the way the family worked"? A fair few of my clients were smacked as children. Pretty regularly. Regularly enough to remember. Some of my clients were beaten at school, with a cane, too. Yet, in most of these cases, the client will say "Oh, but I deserved it. I was being naughty", or "Oh, but that's just how the school operated, and we had to get on with it". And a fair few of my clients have also smacked their children, thinking with their best possible intentions that it was the correct way to discipline a child.

There isn't any crime a child can commit that is worthy of a smack, simply because of the extraordinary effect it has on the child's central nervous system and on their neural pathway connections as they are developing. If smacking is a regular occurrence for a child, if parents use a smack as a way to encourage better behaviour, it is actually causing the reverse as the child grows up. Instead of it helping to raise a "disciplined" child, which of course is the parent's intention, it will, in fact, raise a frightened child who becomes accustomed to living in an over-aroused state with a body full of adrenalin and cortisol. The frightened child is likely to feel unworthy, and not good enough, and will very likely end up using external methods of soothing when they reach their teens and adulthood, if not before, in order to help regulate their heightened central nervous system. Smacking a child has extraordinarily adverse effects on both their physical and emotional growth, and we will look at this more in Chapter 3.

Sexual abuse

Sexual abuse is a Big T trauma. Always. I can't tell you the number of people I meet who say "But I wasn't raped, so it wasn't that bad". Please, please, if you suffered any type of sexually oriented interference when you were little and it has left you feeling "icky" in any way shape or form, this is sexual trauma and it must not be minimised. If it had an effect on you, then we look at it, and we work on it, and we heal it. We don't want you carrying that around anymore. You don't need to be carrying that around anymore. Childhood sexual abuse is any act that is in any way sexual in nature or suggestion, generally performed by anyone at least five years older than us. There is more about this in Chapter 8, but for now, I will say that the misunderstanding around what actually constitutes sexual abuse is both staggering and heartbreaking. And I will hopefully put this misunderstanding to bed in Chapter 8.

Emotional abuse

Emotional abuse is the area where many people lack the education and the knowledge. Not because they don't want to know – on the contrary, think of the amount of parenting books out there on the market – people want to know! The first thing a new parent will most probably do is buy a parenting book of some description. Let's think about that. Why do we buy a parenting book? I just wonder if it's because we don't have 100% faith in how we were parented, and we want to make it better. Remember that niggle I was talking about in the introduction to this chapter? We have a niggle. Yes, we're also overwhelmed with a new baby, overwhelmed to be pregnant, and it's something new and perhaps we're a bit scared. But if we had been parented in the most special way, would we be so anxious to buy a book on parenting? Perhaps, a guide to nappy changes, formula amounts – the practical side. But the parenting book market is way bigger than that, way bigger than just practical advice. And we dive into it head first. Or we're told not to bother, and we don't and we fumble our way through saying "no-one gives you a manual for parenting" – and we still buy a book.

What I have found is that very often parents, teachers or significant adults in our lives end up being the perpetrators of emotional abuse *and they do not even realise they are being abusive and / or neglectful.* If we are already a parent – *we do not realise that we are being abusive and / or neglectful.* Emotional abuse, like physical abuse, is also an attempt to control, but this time through emotional attack, rather than physical attack.

Emotional abuse of a child includes:

- Criticising
- Manipulating
- Favouring one child over another – overtly (obviously) or covertly (in a more hidden way)
- Name-calling
- Swearing, insulting, putting down of a child
- Controlling a child
- Threatening with punishments
- Withholding affection
- Withholding communication (silent treatment)
- Shaming
- Blaming

- Judging
- Shouting at, or raging at a child

Yeah, that's quite a list, isn't it? And yup, they are all emotional abuse.

Emotional neglect

Emotional neglect is all of the above – to be emotionally abusive is very neglectful – but *emotional neglect is also the absence of unconditional love and respect for a child* which is also, of course, the by-product of the emotionally abusive acts listed above.

Bessel van der Kolk, probably the most well-known trauma researcher in the world, in his book *The Body Keeps the Score*, has a chapter on developmental trauma. He calls it "the hidden epidemic" and he is absolutely right, it is hidden and it is an epidemic. Van der Kolk describes appalling cases of youngsters brought to see him, brought up in foster homes, or with addict or alcoholic parents, rife with physical, emotional and sexual abuse as part of their background. When we hear the stories of these children's childhoods, we are shocked, appalled, heartbroken, or even angry that a child can be treated in such a way. Van der Kolk is talking about "overt" physical, sexual and emotional abuse. The children to whom he refers are screamed at regularly, sworn at, hit, raped, not given clean clothes or enough food, nor taken to the doctor when they need it. The abuse here is obvious; even to an untrained person it is clear that these children have been abused and neglected. Bessel put developmental trauma on the map. Thank you, Bessel.

However...

...many of my clients come from lovely families with lots of opportunity. So why do they suffer from developmental trauma?

I look at the majority of my clients. They didn't go from foster home to foster home, they didn't live with parents lost to the depths of addiction, and they weren't necessarily beaten up or raped either. Yet they are suffering from various levels of developmental trauma. What is going on? What are we missing here? What has caused this developmental trauma, when their background and upbringing appears to be relatively privileged and safe?

Emotional abuse and neglect in the spotlight

The missing piece that I witness day, after day, after day, both at work and not at work, is *that there is a staggering misunderstanding around what emotional abuse and neglect really looks like.*

Physical and sexual abuse we are more familiar with – these are technically Big T traumas – but in the mainstream we don't fully understand the depth of emotional abuse and neglect. Since we are talking about developmental trauma, the trauma that occurs in the first 18 years of our lives, *we need to rethink how we understand what constitutes emotional abuse and neglect of children.*

In order to do this, I am going to suggest that we first have a good look at how we were treated as children. So, we're going to move away from my clients for a moment, and we are going to think about ourselves – we are going to have a little think about our own childhood.

To help us, and drawing on the work of Dan Siegel, we are going to think about "4 Ss" as an indicator of how we were really treated and cared for as children – and how we experienced that treatment and care too. These 4 Ss are:

Seen
Soothed
Safe
Secure

As children, from the moment we are conceived and throughout our childhoods, we need to feel Seen, Soothed, Safe and Secure, *enough of the time* and *by enough significant adults around us*, in order that we don't suffer developmental trauma. Or, in order to at least keep the amount of trauma to a minimum.

Let's think about that for ourselves.

Let's think back to when we were little. Let's dig deep and get honest with our most vulnerable self when we ask ourselves these questions.

Seen

When we were younger, in the first 18 years of our life (or the first seven if we are feeling really brave), did we feel Seen?

For example: did we feel that our parents, family members or teachers *knew who we were as an individual*? Did we feel a sense of deep connection with our parents? Did we feel they understood what we were saying, or how we were feeling? And at times when they did not, because their character and generation was different, did we feel that they would then do anything in their power to take the time to listen to us and *to really try to understand us*? That they would carve time out for us to really sit down with us and "get" us? Were we allowed to have an opinion that was ours, even if it differed to that of our parents? Were we respected for our opinion if we were allowed to have one?

Or did we feel that we were simply one of a group, a member of the family, persuaded to adhere to the same values as our parents even if their values didn't feel quite right for us? Did we feel at times (or often) slightly insignificant (or very insignificant), needing to keep our internal world just that – internal.

If we didn't feel Seen, for exactly who we were as an individual, enough of the time, then we will have some developmental trauma.

Soothed

When we think back to our childhood, did we feel there was someone around to Soothe us when we felt down, overwhelmed, angry, sad or emotional? Was there someone who would wrap their arms around us and hold us whilst we experienced whatever emotions were going on for us at the time, without blame, shame or judgement? Were we allowed to be angry? Were we allowed to cry? Were we scooped up and embraced when times got tough or when we had a challenge?

Or were we told – or did we get the vibe that we had to – "be quiet", or "just get on with it", or "buck up and cheer up", or "our family doesn't get angry", or "big girls don't cry"?

If we were a boy, were we even allowed to cry, or were we told: "boys don't cry"?

If we didn't feel soothed enough in our childhood, then we will have some developmental trauma.

Safe

Did we feel Safe? Provided we didn't have a physically abusive parent, we hopefully felt physically safe most of the time. But did we feel emotionally safe? Did we feel that we could go to our parents or caregivers or teachers or other adults in our life and tell them exactly how we were feeling at any moment in time? Were we encouraged to do this? Were we allowed to express our anger? Were we allowed an opinion? Were we allowed to have a darn good cry when we needed? Or were we discouraged from doing this? Did we feel Seen and Soothed? Did we feel we could trust our parents with how we were feeling, and that we could take anything – anything to them that came up for us that was uncomfortable? Or were we scared or worried that they would be cross, uninterested, unsympathetic or shaming?

If we didn't feel emotionally Safe, enough of the time, then we will have some developmental trauma.

Secure

Our sense of security very often comes from learning that Mum and Dad will mess up, but that when they do, they will repair. No parent is perfect – and isn't expected to be, that would probably be a trauma for a child in and of itself. So our sense of security will come from knowing that when Mum and Dad mess up, they will apologise and repair, and that will make us feel secure.

If we didn't feel Secure, enough of the time, then we will have some developmental trauma.

For those of you who have answered "yes, I had those 4 Ss!", I am really glad for you.

Very sadly, you are a minority.

If we know deep down that we did not get all of those 4 Ss enough, when we were growing up, then we have unresolved developmental trauma.

And... if we did not receive those 4 Ss enough, then we experienced a sense of emotional abuse and neglect.

Let's look more deeply at the clients I mentioned above.

Clare, who came to me because her marriage was in crisis, was constantly anxious, wracked with guilt, and looking forward too much to her daily evening drink. By her definition, she had lived a really privileged life, with a "gorgeous and happy childhood" (her words). When I explained the 4 Ss to her, she started to cry. She had been sent to boarding school aged eight, cried for two weeks and been shamed by the matrons for being homesick. She had had a very bright older sister whom she had never felt good enough around. Her parents disallowed their children to express anger and tears, and she didn't even remember ever getting a hug from her mum. She loved her dad, but he had been partially absent due to his work, and she'd been at home with a stony cold mum and her siblings for most of her formative years. She realised she had never felt seen for who she truly was, didn't really reckon she'd been soothed when she'd needed it, and certainly didn't feel emotionally safe. And she had never had an apology from a parent. So, all four of those 4 Ss were missing from her childhood.

Belinda, who came to see me because she didn't know how to be around her children without feeling angry with them, faced the sad truth that the separation of her parents when she was five years old had, in fact, left her feeling livid with her parents and with the world. But she hadn't been encouraged to talk about her feelings at all as a child – her mother was even known to say things like "Nobody cares how you feel, just get on with it". So she swallowed her anger and continued through life. But when she had her own children, this repressed anger erupted and she occasionally took it out on her children. Belinda had not felt Seen, Soothed, Safe or Secure.

Rebecca came to see me because she couldn't stand being in the same room as her sister and always felt walked over and trodden on, and she had no idea how to stop this happening. When we started to talk about the 4 Ss, she looked at me shocked "But I didn't get any of them!" she said. She is not alone.

Sarah, who came because her mother was continuing to take over her life, even though she was now 45 years old, couldn't stand it any longer. When we explored her childhood, we discovered that her mum was grossly narcissistic a lot of the time, seeing her children as clones of her and not allowing them to express their own personal needs at all. Anyone with a narcissistic mum will have had a pretty full-on absence of the 4 Ss, for sure.

Sometimes, a client will arrive and, after a couple of history-taking sessions, I will see glaringly that there is no way this person received enough of the 4 Ss, yet they will not be able to see it themselves. This is when the absence of love and respect is so normalised within the family system that the client still, as an adult, cannot see that they didn't receive what they needed, and what they deserved. Heather, for example, couldn't believe what I was talking about when I asked her if she had been hugged as a child.

"Hugged?" she asked me. "No way. Our family didn't do hugs. We never used the word 'love' either, ew, gross".

This absence of love was so normalised within Heather's family that it made her physically recoil to even think of it.

Very often too, I will see a client from a family of such high-functioning dysfunction that the client has a deep, deep belief that they are not deserving of the 4 Ss. The message they received during their life was "you are not worthy of love". The start of the work here is gently convincing the client that they are just as worthy of love as anyone else in the world because, until they realise that, they will continue to suffer their panic attacks, or their addictions, or their depression, or their anxiety (or whatever their struggle might be) in their adult life. Trauma work will be more challenging for them until they can open, even just a little, to the notion that it is OK for them to be able to accept love.

When there is a lack of love and respect and 4 Ss within the family system as a whole, very often the client – even as an adult – will view the notion of the 4 Ss as "cissy", or "fluffy", or "unnecessary". This is the greatest tragedy of all, and this contributes to the normalisation of trauma and its repercussions, which I will discuss in more detail later in the book.

Emotional attunement

"Emotional attunement" needs to be in place in order that we avoid any emotional abuse and neglect. In order for a child to grow up into a fully functioning, emotionally whole grown-up, they need a parent who is emotionally attuned to them – enough of the time. What do I mean by emotional attunement? In essence, it is being aware of someone's inner, personal emotional experience, and allowing them to feel it and process it, within the safety confines of age-appropriate, behavioural boundaries.

Explaining emotional attunement to a client once, they asked "Yeah, but isn't that what I come to therapy for?" To which my response was "Yes, of course, but if you had received it during childhood from your significant others then you probably wouldn't be needing therapy". This lady was so unaccustomed to the feeling of someone understanding her that she honestly thought it was only available in a therapeutic space.

The tragedy here is that these clients are not alone.

When this unconditional emotional attunement is available from the parent, it provides an automatic connection from parent to child, which allows the child to feel safe, loved, understood, respected, and treasured (Safe, Seen, Soothed and Secure) for exactly who they are, and how they are, at any given moment. In other words, this emotional attunement by the parent fulfils all the needs of the child. When the adult welcomes, permits, embraces and accepts the child, regardless of what is going on for the parent at the time, every single part of this child grows and develops, and this child matures naturally into an emotionally whole adult.

But sadly, most children do not receive this. Many of us did not receive this.

This lack of emotional attunement by parents ends up with the child's needs not being met, and this results in developmental trauma. We look more at emotional attunement, what interrupts it and why this is, in Chapter 4.

> *We lack awareness around the importance*
> *of emotional attunement.*

When there is a lack of emotional attunement, a child quickly works out what parents can and cannot tolerate, and changes him or herself accordingly, in order to be "approved of" (aka loved) by the parent.

What we need most, as a child, is to feel a connection with our parents or primary caregiver. If the primary caregiver is not emotionally attuned to us as a child, then the caregiver does not automatically forge that connection with us.

We need so badly to feel connected that we will then change ourselves, unconsciously, to fit with the caregiver in order to feel that sense of connection.

Put another way, instead of the caregiver fulfilling our needs as a child, we learn quickly – and unconsciously – how to fulfil our caregiver's needs. This is completely and utterly the wrong way around, yet it happens all the time – without us knowing it – because we just don't know this stuff, we are not taught it. But the importance of feeling connected to our parents is one on of the most, if not the most, important thing we strive for as children.

Unmet needs in childhood = developmental trauma.

This lack of emotional attunement from our parent is a form of emotional neglect. Yes, that does sound harsh, but this is not a judgement – we simply do not know about this stuff. And because we don't know about this stuff:

We were traumatised as children without realising it, and we are traumatising our children without knowing it.

Until we have done lots of trauma work, or we have a client come into our office unable to sustain a healthy adult relationship because of their "wine o'clock" habit and inability to internally self-soothe, and we discover that they are reliving the trauma of not being picked up from their cot when they were crying pre aged three (for example – it could be because of any number of unmet needs from childhood), one cannot know. How can we?

Many people simply have not, in the past, been educated adequately on the importance of emotional attunement to a child.

Diana came to see me because she had ended an affair with a married man a few months before, and she felt as though she was falling apart. She knew, in her head, that the affair needed to end – the man in question had decided to go back to his wife and work on their marriage – yet she felt broken inside, desperate, abandoned, and grieving, still, months after the relationship had ended. In the session, she effortlessly traced these feelings of desperation and loss around the break-up back to being young enough to be lying in a cot unable to move herself, crying and crying and crying and crying – with no-one coming to get her. It also went back to her being dropped off at school without Mummy saying goodbye, because the teachers advised that it was better for the child if there were no goodbyes at drop off. And it also went back to her deep sense of feeling emotionally abandoned by her mum who simply wasn't in touch with her own feelings as a mother, and who was therefore not able to forge that unconditional emotional attunement with her daughter. Once we had processed these events – and a few more similar to that, and "mended" them – healed them – she no longer experienced the level of emotional pain around the break-up of the affair. The break-up of the affair had triggered her own childhood abandonment wounds which were a result of her not having parents who were emotionally attuned enough to her needs.

As other case studies throughout this book will show, for a child to not have their needs met – for them to not receive enough of the 4 Ss enough of the time – feels, to that child, as if they are being abandoned and rejected on a regular basis.

And this results in unprocessed trauma that we unknowingly carry into our adult lives.

Developmental deficit

When we don't receive enough of the 4 Ss in those early years, we get left with what we refer to as a "developmental deficit". In other words, something missing from our journey through development – a missing "need", results in a deficit in our development. A developmental deficit is just a fancy way (and slightly quicker way) of saying "the gap that's left inside us because of an unmet need".

Sometimes this deficit is a result of horrible things happening, and our having to block them out, because there was no-one there to adequately help us through these events. But sometimes too – and much more often – it is simply a result of us not getting enough of what we really needed.

Both of these outcomes are the result of emotional neglect.

If we were emotionally abused or neglected, we will have a developmental deficit and we will have some developmental trauma.

When we are small, when we have a disrupted attachment with our primary caregivers, we will unconsciously and automatically find ourselves in a full-on survival mode much of the time (more on this in Chapter 3). We go into survival mode when we feel we are in danger, or when there is a threat. And for a child, not having a secure enough attachment with a caregiver, suffering any type of abuse or neglect, or not feeling Seen, Soothed, Safe, or Secure enough of the time, will feel like the most life threatening thing on earth.

We do not want to minimise the impact that Big T traumas can have on us, but we absolutely have to pay more attention to the impact of developmental trauma. Because it is very often these Little T trauma wounds that run most deeply and that are the most painful and difficult for us to heal.

The next chapter will look at the detrimental effects of this emotional abuse and neglect, and the ensuing developmental deficit. It will also look in more detail at ways that we have become traumatised.

CHAPTER 2

A direct route to the past

In Chapter 1 we looked at trauma being the result of something horrid happening to us, or something loving not happening enough for us, and how that leaves us with trauma and a developmental deficit – or unprocessed emotions and unmet childhood needs. This chapter will look at how we adapt in order to cope with our unresolved trauma. It will also look at how and when our trauma resurfaces in our daily life, namely in the form of triggers – which I will explain fully later in the chapter. Understanding this is imperative to really grasping the depth of the trauma epidemic.

Trauma is "wounding"

A trauma is a like a wound – it is a wound. Trauma is essentially wounding. It feels wounding. It hurts.

In the same way that a physical wound can be enormous or slight, an emotional wound can be enormous or slight too. Just as a physical wound can hurt like hell or just be sore, an emotional wound can also hurt like hell – or it can simply "hurt".

No-one can go through their lives without feeling hurt from someone. Feeling hurt is part of life and part of being human, and part of human relationships of every sort – parental, sibling, co-worker, teacher or romantic. And of course, there are many, many hurts that we can – and do – recover from, on our own, throughout our lives, on a regular basis. But whether we manage to work through and "process" hurt, rather than pushing it away under the carpet and pretending it didn't hurt, depends on many factors. These include what event or experience this hurt came from, who hurt us, how frequently it happened, how sensitive we are, what other hurts we also have, our character make-up, how that hurt was dealt with at the time, and also whether our family system recognised and acknowledged our hurt as even qualifying as a hurt. All of these factors contribute to whether the trauma gets lodged as an unprocessed event – an unprocessed hurt – or not.

Many of us push our hurts away and pretend they didn't happen. It is important that we ask ourselves the question "did I actually recover from that wounding, or did I merely push the hurt away and *pretend* that it didn't hurt so much because that is what I needed to do in order to survive?"

This is a very, very important question. Because if we are pretending it didn't hurt, then we haven't processed it and it will be affecting our behaviours in our current lives.

Pretending traumas don't hurt, or "adapting" ourselves to the hurt, is massively epidemic and is one of the reasons our trauma goes unnoticed for so long.

How trauma can present itself

Some of you might be reading this book and already be thinking "Wow, I have trauma, and I didn't know it". Others of you might be asking yourselves "How do I know I have trauma? How can I tell if I've pushed a hurt away or if I've processed it?"

Here's a very simple little exercise that can help us to find the answers to these questions.

Think back through your life. Just do a scan. Are there any events, or things that happened, that when you think of them now, still carry a negative emotional charge? In other words, do you have any memories from the past that still feel difficult or painful when you recall them?

Any events from the past that still carry an emotional charge for us are unresolved traumas.

You might think back to that scary teacher who didn't like you. Or perhaps being dropped off at school. Or some mean kids at school in the playground. Or a parental separation / divorce. Or the birth of a sibling. Or threats of punishment when you were little. Or your parents arguing, or your parents going away from home for an extended amount of time. Or those times you stole chocolate and received a smack.

Some people, on the other hand, cannot think of anything troubling from the past. Not one thing. There are two possible reasons for this. Either we have minimised the past event and have become so adapted that we can't connect with it emotionally at all, or, we have blocked it out of our memory bank completely.

Numbness is an emotional charge. We just can't feel it, so it doesn't feel like one. Numbness is different from "neutral". If we recall a past event and we feel emotionally neutral around it, we have most probably processed it. But if we feel "numb", then we have not.

Sometimes I ask a client to tell me about their childhood and their response is "I really can't remember that much". This is a sure sign to me that there is developmental trauma there. Why is this? Because when we can't remember much of the past, it is because the experiences were so painful, from the standpoint of our child self, that we had to block them off in order to continue with life; literally block them off in our minds and in our hearts. We will look at why we do this more fully in Chapter 4.

But for now, let's look at what happens to us, in our adult lives, when we are carrying anything unresolved from the past.

Below are lists of symptoms of trauma. I have started with the more well-known ones.

Well-known symptoms of trauma:

- Addictions
- Food disorders
- Depression
- Anxiety
- Antisocial behaviour

- Borderline personality disorder
- Attention deficit hyperactivity disorder (ADHD)
- Attention deficit disorder (ADD)
- Smoking
- Suicide attempts
- Sexual promiscuity
- Criminal activity
- Agoraphobia
- Panic attacks
- Flashbacks
- Recurring nightmares

For many people, certainly in terms of the presentations listed above, there is a nameable and often overtly noticeable "problem" that is obviously affecting us and our lives. In other words, people tend to notice, for example, when someone is in a deep depression, or having panic attacks, or steeped in addiction.

Many of you suffering from those symptoms listed above might not realise you have unresolved trauma. You do.

But for others, the symptoms are not as overt or obvious as those listed above:

Less well-known signs of trauma:

- Feeling negatively towards oneself
- Feeling "something's not quite right"
- Passivity
- Not able to speak up for oneself

- People-pleasing
- Caretaking – constantly putting others' needs before our own
- Being a doormat
- Not speaking our truth
- Imposter syndrome
- Feeling responsible for everything and everyone
- Reaching for something external to make one feel better
- Stuck in relationships we are not happy in
- Feelings of "should" or "ought"
- Sense of entitlement
- Arrogance or grandiosity
- Narcissism
- Stream of unfulfilling relationships
- Feelings of shame
- Irrational fears
- Constant feeling of loneliness
- Uncontrollable anger
- Fear of being abandoned by another person or group
- Finding it difficult to say "no"
- Always being the one to pick up the pieces
- Jealousy of others and their lives
- Inability to be alone with oneself
- Always needing to be busy
- Inability to set boundaries
- Inability to accept others' boundaries
- Feelings of numbness
- Inability to connect with our feelings
- Only able to have fun with alcohol (or drugs)
- Only able to have sex with alcohol (or drugs)
- Obsession with health

- Feeling "everything will be OK once I feel better about myself physically"
- Flying into rages
- Constant irritabilities about everyday life

It's a pretty long list, isn't it? And it's not exhaustive either.

All of the above are symptoms of something – or some things – from the past that have not been processed. These can be either events, a lack of the 4 Ss, or both. As a general rule, the greater number and magnitude of symptoms in adulthood, the more unresolved trauma we have.

Any type of trauma, Big T or Little T, will result in some sort of discomfort in our adult lives, because the physiology (i.e. what's going on in the brain and the body) behind trauma *is exactly the same* if we witness our best friend being blown up in Iraq, if we blow up our best friend in Iraq, if we were bullied at school, if we were physically abused, if we were told by our parent "boys don't cry", if we had an alcoholic parent, or if we grew up with an emotionally distant parent. Regardless of what the traumatic event or experience was, *the physiology in the brain is exactly the same* (more on this in Chapter 3).

All of the events above, despite how different they might appear in terms of intensity and presentation, if not fully processed at the time, will result in us having unresolved trauma.

And the physiology behind trauma is the physiology behind trauma, no matter what the event or experience.

How can we be absolutely sure that we have unresolved trauma?

So we've seen the list of symptoms above, and I've told you that if you have any of them then you have unresolved trauma. But some of you perhaps don't want to believe me. That's OK.

Some people know they have trauma. And some people looking at the lists above will hopefully now go and get trauma therapy and be relieved of those uncomfortable, limiting behaviours, that no longer serve them.

But many, many people with less obvious and / or acute or overt symptoms (but symptoms nonetheless) do not realise that they have trauma. This will result in us suffering in silence. Sometimes, we will feel too ashamed even to admit that we can't really cope with something, and that we are not really happy with ourselves or with our lives.

Any childhood devoid of enough of the 4 Ss will put stress on a child. If this tension is not resolved during our childhood, it will result in post-traumatic stress that will continue into our adult life, most probably manifesting as one or more of the behaviours listed above, that will persist until it has been recognised and treated.

Negative self-beliefs / feeling negatively towards oneself

If we have negative beliefs about ourselves,
we are carrying unresolved trauma.

One of the items on the earlier list of less-known trauma symptoms is "feeling negatively towards oneself". This deserves its own exploration in more detail. Because another tell-tale sign that we have unresolved trauma – for either Big T or developmental trauma – is that we have a negative view about ourselves, or the world.

These negative views revolve around four main themes. A notion of self-defectiveness – there is something wrong with me. A sense of responsibility – it's all my fault, everything is up to me to sort out. Around safety – I don't feel safe, I am alone. Around choice – I am powerless to change anything, I am completely stuck. And personal power – I cannot succeed, I can't stand up for myself, I am helpless.

Here is a more comprehensive list of what are termed "negative cognitions", or negative beliefs about ourselves:

I am not good enough – I am a bad person – I don't deserve love – I am not lovable – I am inadequate – I am worthless – I am weak – I am permanently damaged – I am shameful – I am not worthy of success – I am not worth it – I am defective – I deserve to die – I am stupid – I am a failure – I am different – I don't belong – I am alone

I should have done something – I should have known better – I should have done more – I did something wrong – It's my fault – I cannot be trusted – My best is not good enough – I am to blame

I am not safe – I can't trust anyone – I am in danger – I can't protect myself – I am going to die – It's not OK to feel or show my emotions – It's not OK to be me – I cannot trust myself – I am not safe – I cannot show my emotions – I am alone

I am not in control – I am powerless – I am helpless – I am weak – I cannot trust myself – I cannot control my life – I have to please everyone – I am trapped – I have no options

Let's have a look at those statements above. We might want to tweak the wording to make them more personal to ourselves, and that's a good thing to do, but however we choose to word them, most of us carry some – or a lot – of these beliefs around with us on a daily basis. Some of us will encounter these beliefs in certain situations and not others. However frequently or infrequently we have these beliefs about ourselves, they are an indication that we carry unresolved trauma. Often when I show clients this list of negative chatter, they say they experience a great deal – if not all – of these phrases at some point or other. Sometimes people feel relieved when they realise that there are a few phrases that are absolutely *not* true for them, once they realise how much negative chatter they are carrying around inside them – and believing.

Sometimes these negative cognitions are referred to as "limiting beliefs". And indeed they are, because they "limit" our ability to thrive.

One client, upon looking at the list of negative beliefs that I'd showed her, looked at me and said, "But doesn't everyone have these beliefs about themselves?" And I'm afraid the answer is yes, most people do, if they haven't yet done the work on themselves. This lady was implying that surely it's OK to feel like this about ourselves, because everyone else does as well.

Of course we can choose to hold on to these beliefs about ourselves if we wish to, but we absolutely do not have to. It is possible to change them permanently by doing some deep, inner work on ourselves.

Because none of these beliefs are actually true for us at all, even though they sure as hell *feel* true.

Adaptations to trauma are simply our "protection"

All of the ways in which we adapt to our trauma, in other words all of these symptoms of trauma, are in fact our brain and body's incredibly clever and sophisticated way of protecting us.

We are protecting ourselves - albeit unconsciously - from the deeply painful and overwhelming feelings that have been blocked off, or shoved away. When we reach for something external to soothe us, be it a person, a cigarette, an alcoholic drink, food, shopping, or even depression, we are protecting ourselves from the pain of what either happened to us, or didn't happen for us, in the past.

When we are little, it is simply too much to process at the time that Mummy isn't emotionally available, or that Daddy shouts when he's had too many drinks, or the terror and shame around the cane from the headmaster, or the angry teacher who makes us feel stupid, or the threats of punishment if we aren't "good", so we do not process these events or experiences. We block them off. We shut them down.

But they continue to play out unconsciously in our adult lives, only in a different way. To continue to believe we are not good enough, for example, keeps us from having to feel the pain of not feeling good enough. This might look like staying in a job that we are bored in, feeling not good enough to try to change our job. The staying in the job protects us from the fear of facing the horror of wounds from the past, where we learned the negative cognition "I am not good enough".

All of these symptoms of trauma are methods of self-protection. They might look like self-sabotage, because they can be so damaging to us, but they are all in fact methods of self-protection. We are protecting ourselves from deep, deep hurts.

Sometimes too, we reach for the external "things" in order to hide the fact that we feel so badly towards ourselves. We have a drink to curb anxiety or "take the edge off" the stress of the day. We choose a husband or wife who will protect us financially because we don't feel able to provide for ourselves. We have an affair because we are too frightened to confront our other half and tell them that our needs are not being met in our relationship. We excuse our angry outbursts towards our children, blaming them for their "bad" behaviour, when actually our outburst is centred around us not feeling like a good enough parent, because we don't feel good enough in our core.

We adapt, in order that we do not have to face our own buried wounds.

Triggers

To finish this chapter we need to talk about triggers. "Triggering" has become a bit of a buzzword of late. This is fantastic – so long as it lasts – and so long as it's used in the correct context.

So, what does it mean to be triggered? What is a trigger?

Our triggers are gifts.

I call triggers "gifts", because in the work that I do, we often use triggers to take us directly to the core trauma, and then we can heal the trauma – and we are no longer triggered! Wahoo! So I love triggers. They don't feel so good, in fact they can feel like hell don't get me wrong, but bear with me, and hopefully you'll appreciate them soon, too.

Triggers can be slight or they can be gigantic, and they can be every intensity in between. Have you ever said or thought the phrase "she / he presses my buttons"? That's you being triggered. Do you ever feel constant irritation about small, everyday things like a clock ticking? That's you being triggered. Sometimes triggers are huge. Do you ever fly into a moment of rage? That's you being triggered. Something might happen, perhaps you make a mistake at work, and you go into a deep terror. That's you being triggered.

Essentially, a trigger can be a person, situation, opinion, word, tone of voice, smell, material thing, or place – in other words anything at all – that provokes an emotional reaction inside us, usually along the lines of rage, fear, terror, anxiety, panic, sadness, grief or loss. Triggers can be conscious or unconscious.

Many of us are triggered pretty often without even realising that it is happening.

Sometimes, when we are triggered, we go straight into our self-protection behaviour without even feeling any of the triggered feelings. For example, we find ourselves standing in front of the open fridge wondering what to eat half an hour after we've finished supper and we don't know why. Or we receive a text that we don't like, and we reflexively pour ourselves a glass of wine. Or we see that our significant other is in a bad mood and immediately put on a smile to prevent them flaring up further. Or we constantly, and without much consideration, reply with a yes, when we really want to say no, because we are frightened of upsetting others.

How severely we are triggered is on a spectrum. Someone might say something, or something might happen, and we might feel a bit knocked over emotionally, or we might feel as though we've been stabbed. On the other end of the spectrum, we might experience a feeling of utter panic, terror, rage or intense grief. These are all signs that we have been triggered, however large or small.

If it's "hysterical", it's "historical".

There is an expression that has been used for decades and it states: "If it's hysterical it's historical". It is not the most lovely of expressions (any anti-misogynist will probably detest it), but it is very good at helping us to work out when our present-day reactions are triggering something from the past.

Essentially, if we feel we are "overreacting" to something that has happened in that moment – in other words, if our reaction is "hysterical" – then in that moment we are being triggered.

Because in that moment, what is actually happening is that one or more of our past wounds – our unprocessed traumas – is being opened.

Another way of looking at whether we are being triggered, or whether we are having an appropriate, grown-up reaction, is to use a scale of 1-10 to describe the intensity of our feelings. If something happens and we feel anger on the 1-5 end of the scale, then we are probably feeling appropriate anger for the situation. But if we feel rage, this is on the 5-10 end of the scale and we are being triggered. If we feel anxious before we give a public talk, we could describe this anxiety as on the 1-5 end of the scale. If we feel panic before we give a talk, however, and this panic is clearly on the 5-10 end of the scale, then the fear of public speaking is triggering a past, unhealed wound.

When we are triggered, we are taken right back into an unhealed wound from the past, and in that moment, that past wound is reopened.

Often this is only a temporary opening up of a wound – and then it closes again. We feel rage in that moment, but then we calm down later. For parents reading this, think bath time at the end of a long day and Little Jonny refuses to brush his teeth. You are hungry, tired, the dog needs feeding, downstairs is a mess that you know you need to tidy later, and on Little Jonny's fourth "NO!" you feel the rage surging inside you. You have been triggered. We are more open to being triggered when we are feeling vulnerable and tired. You might lash out at Jonny, you might not. You might take some time to calm down – you might stay uptight until you've had a glass of wine later (reaching for external substances). But you have been triggered.

A businessman, who holds a lot of his self-worth in his income that he brings to the family, suddenly is told he might lose his job. He becomes frightened and panicky, acting out, grumpy, unable to sleep well, worried, snapping at family members. Of course there will be worry when there is job loss, this is natural. However, feelings on the 5-10 end of the scale – like terror, panic, insomnia, fear, lashing out – this is more than just an adult worry about job loss. This is a sign that this businessman has been triggered into a past wound (or past wounds) by the threat of losing his job.

Triggers can also open past wounds for a longer period of time. For example, we receive a harsh comment from our ageing mother, and we feel wobbly for a few days or even weeks afterwards. Or we receive harsh criticism from a colleague or boss, and we feel worthless for a few days (or longer). Or we really do lose that job, and we feel as though our whole world and sense of worth has vanished into thin air.

Sometimes we are triggered right back to the traumatising memory itself. For example, Leslie, aged 28, had been in a horrible car crash in her teens. For many years, she didn't think about the crash at all, but when she turned 24 she suddenly started having flashbacks to the crash whenever she was stuck in a traffic jam. The traffic jam was triggering her trauma from her car crash. We have probably heard about soldiers coming back from war zones and feeling jumpy then panicking when they hear a car backfiring – or fireworks. There are some

World War II survivors who still hate fireworks, because they are reminded of noises they heard in the war; this is their unresolved war trauma being triggered by the fireworks.

Very often, though, we do not get triggered into the actual trauma memory. Rob, 42, is an active father of three children, who are all below the age of six. He came to see me because he would fly into an internal rage whenever his children whinged or whined, or when they cried for a prolonged period. He said that when they were babies, on some days he actually wanted to shake them to stop them crying. He felt so ashamed about feeling this way even though he knew he would never follow through on his impulse to shake them. Sometimes he would inflict this rage on his children by yelling at them, but sometimes he would rage internally, simply becoming snappy to all of those around him, and would then go to the pub and have a few pints to calm down. He didn't recall any childhood event whilst he was feeling so rageful, but we did the work together, and Rob discovered that, during these times with his children, he was actually being triggered right back to early emotional memories of his father who was overly strict with him. His father wouldn't allow him to cry when he was a child, and his mother was passive and simply looked on whilst his father maintained strict discipline. Rob did the trauma work, and allowed himself to cry and cry and cry in his sessions. By doing the trauma work, he rewired his younger brain so that it was permitted to cry, assuring the younger Rob that his cries would now be heard and listened to, and comforted. He released all of these tears and other trapped emotions in the sessions. He is no longer triggered by his children crying, and instead he scoops them up into his arms and hugs them. His relationship with his children has improved a thousandfold.

Louise, 54, couldn't stop crying for months after her husband left her. She thought that this was all about her grief around losing her husband. Some of it was, but unbeknown to her, she had also been triggered into the abandonment she had felt as a child from having a mother who was not emotionally available to her enough of the time. When Louise's husband left her, a deep wound was opened. This wound originated from her pre-seven-year-old self who had felt abandoned by her mother – the person she had needed to feel (and should have felt) safe with. We did a few sessions on Louise's childhood, desensitising all of those feelings of abandonment and loss around her mother, and during the processing we gave that little Louise everything she needed (most of the 4 Ss) that she hadn't received at the time. Once we had finished the work, she was no longer crying over her marriage. She realised completely that it was not all about her husband leaving her at all, but much more about her younger self that had been triggered and the unconscious abandonment memories that had been imprinted on her child psyche and carried forward into her adult experiences.

In addition to the strong emotions that come up when we are triggered, there can also be physical signs. These can include shaking, palpitations / heart racing, a choking feeling, trouble breathing or swallowing, hot flushes or chills, feeling dizzy, feeling nauseous, pain in the chest or belly or solar plexus, going numb, or feeling unreal (also known as detachment or dissociation). Very often, it is these latter feelings – going numb and dissociating – that lead us to act out immediately on our self-soothing strategies to supress our trauma symptoms.

For so many of us, though, it is the simple "he / she really pushes my buttons..." that shows how we are triggered so often, without even realising it.

Lora is a 49-year-old florist, and she came to see me because, in her words, "my colleague at work really presses my buttons, and it's become so uncomfortable being at work, it's like I can't stand her – in fact, I can't stand her". This colleague of Lora's was triggering her into past events that Lora didn't even realise were problematic for her – and totally unrelated to her work as a florist.

How does triggering take us back into old wounds?

So how does this notion of triggering take us back into old, unprocessed material? Let's imagine that an invisible, but functional, pipe runs right down into a past wound. In the moment that we are triggered, it is as though the lid has been lifted on that wound, and all of the repressed emotions from the wound shoot up the pipe and into our body. Whoa. Yeah. Tidal wave in that moment.

Hence "hysterical". Hence 5-10 on the feeling intensity spectrum.

We don't need to know what the past traumatic events were before we start the trauma work. If we are being triggered, that invisible (but functional) pipe will lead us right to the memory connected to the trigger.

You can see for yourself right now.

Have a go at this short exercise below, and see what happens. This is the technique that I use with clients in order to find past trauma targets to process.

If you have a lot of unresolved trauma, and you sort of sense it, or you know it, then don't do this exercise. Instead, please find a lovely trauma therapist with whom you can do this exercise – and also find some resolution in the session.

Drop back in time exercise

1. Think back, over the past week or so, and think of something that you found difficult. It doesn't matter what. It might be a conversation with your mother on the telephone, a difficult moment with your children when you felt your buttons being pushed, an altercation with a partner or an ex-partner, or a difficult moment at work when your boss put you down. Perhaps you felt manipulated by a co-worker, or even annoyance at the barista in a coffee shop one morning. You choose. But choose something relatively small.

2. Once you have chosen, close your eyes and just run the video of what happened in your mind – play it over again and notice how you are feeling. For example, reimagine seeing your mother's number come up on the screen of your phone – notice how you felt then... picking up and having a conversation, then a bit of the conversation irking you – notice how you felt then. Also notice, as you run this video, which part of the memory feels as though it gives you the strongest reaction in this moment as you recall it now. Once you have found that moment of strong reaction (any one of them will do), freeze that frame. Freeze it into a still picture, as though you were going to send it to me as a postcard. Good.

3. Now you have this freeze-frame of the image that impacted you the most, notice what you are feeling. Keep your eyes closed. Then notice where this feeling is in your body. Is it in your gut? Your chest? In the middle? Everywhere? Arms? Back of your neck? Just notice what's going on in your body.

4. Next, ask yourself "What do I believe about myself in this moment?". Again, with your eyes still closed, and as you imagine the image, noticing those feelings attached to it, feeling what you feel, just in this moment – what do you believe about yourself? Think back to the earlier list of negative cognitions and see what fits for you in this moment. It will usually begin with "I am..." and then a negative belief. I am unsafe, I am not heard, I am unlovable, I am worthless, I am powerless. You choose the negative belief that fits best with this moment.

5. Now, with your eyes still closed, take that image, those feelings, those body sensations and that belief, and drop back in time, as far as you can go, without censoring it. *Don't try, just allow. Be curious. Observe. Trust the process.*

6. See what comes up. Something will. And it will most probably be from pretty far back in the past.

Whatever has come up for you is an unhealed wound.

When we do trauma work, this is one of the ways in which we find the core wounds from the past that need healing, the implicit memories that are stored as wounded events or experiences, that are still driving our thoughts and behaviours and feelings in the present.

Throughout the remainder of the book, there are case studies demonstrating healing from past expereinces. In each of these case studies, in the session, this "drop back in time" exercise is used to find the core wound needing to be healed.

The next chapter looks at what is going on in the brain when events from the past are not fully processed, and how this can result in us having residual trauma.

CHAPTER 3

Trauma and the brain

We have an automatic, unconscious and physiological reaction to a threat of any kind – be it a threat that is real, or merely perceived.

By now, we will have an understanding of what trauma is, and what our symptoms of trauma can look like. Hopefully we can now see that we all have at least a little stuck from the past (who doesn't?). We might even be realising quite how much is holding us back from really living and experiencing our lives to the fullest.

This chapter looks at what is going on in the brain when past events get stuck. Why and how do these memories get stuck? Why don't they just get processed at the time?

In order to answer these questions, it is really helpful to understand, at a very basic level, and with the help of metaphors, what is going on in the brain.

Let's think about how the brain works, all day every day, to process events and experiences.

The brain consists of hundreds of billions of neural pathways connecting with each other all of the time.

"Neurons that fire together, wire together"
— Donald O. Hebb

As we learn new information throughout our lives, neural pathways in our brains form connections which enable that information to be retained. This might be as simple as learning what a house is, so that when we see a house we can recognise it as a house: our neural pathways have already connected to recognise a house when we see one.

These neural pathways can offer us the gift of lovely associations. For example, hearing a piece of music that reminds us of happy times, can make us feel happy every time we listen to that piece of music.

But the same principle applies when we have had more difficult, or more traumatic, experiences. Our neural pathways will connect accordingly.

For the sake of understanding trauma healing from the perspective of Eye Movement Desensitisation and Reprocessing (EMDR), the healing modality used with the case studies in this book, we can use the metaphor of the brain being in two parts.

We are going to call these parts the "right brain" and the "left brain" (see diagram).

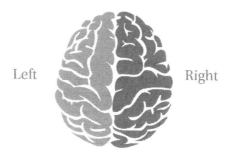

Left   Right

We are going to imagine our right brain as our "feelings" brain. It is our creative side, our intuition, and the more artistic side of our brain. It is where our limbic system is situated, and it houses our feelings and emotions.

We are going to imagine our left brain as our "thinking" brain. It is rational and logical. It makes sense of things and is predominantly our prefrontal cortex.

Here is a little diagram to help us visualise the metaphor of the right and left brain:

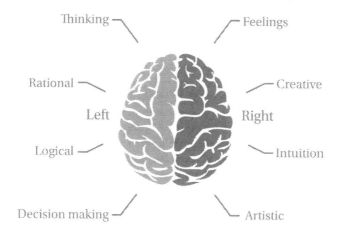

Thinking   Feelings

Rational   Creative

Left   Right

Logical   Intuition

Decision making   Artistic

ıething happens in our day that is not emotionally
ıe information enters our left brain, our thinking
ɒıaın. ɼor example, we might be about to cross the road.
We look both ways, we see there are no cars coming, and our
left brain works out, with its logic, reasoning and rationalising
powers, that it is safe for us to cross the road. So we do cross the
road and all is good.

However, let's imagine something happens that is a bit more
emotionally charged.

Imagine we're about to cross the road, and perhaps our mind
is elsewhere, and we forget to look both ways. We step out into
the road at the exact same moment that a car coming towards
us speeds up. We hear the car and see it coming towards us!
What do we feel? Panic! Fear! We quickly jump back on to
the pavement, and the car speeds on. We're not hurt. We're
safe. We calm right down, and we cross the road. We carry on
our way and, a few minutes later, we're most likely not even
thinking about the car anymore – in fact, we probably won't
give the incident a moment's thought ever again. This is an
example of how we feel afterwards, when our brain completely
processes an emotionally charged event; in other words, we're
OK. We don't give the episode another thought because it has
been fully processed and consequently left in the past, exactly
where it should be.

Fight or flight

You might have heard of "fight" or "flight". They are our first two
trauma responses. Let's see how they fit with our car incident.

The very moment we see / hear the car, we jump back on to the pavement. It is the "flight" trauma response that has caused us to jump back on to the pavement. We didn't need to hang around and fight the car, we just "flighted" out of the way.

Freeze

Now let's imagine we cross the road, and we get to the middle of the road. Suddenly, we look and realise there is a car hurtling towards us. Utter terror! Then we "freeze". We find we are rooted to the spot, and we can't move. The brain has worked out that fight (attack the car) or flight (run away) aren't going to work here, there's no time, so it goes to another response which is "freeze". We still might be OK; the car might brake, skid and swerve. But imagine it doesn't and we're hit. We might then stay in the freeze state, because we are still very much in a trauma response – the trauma of being hit by a car, is, after all, still occurring.

Let's think back to the first example where we just step out on to the road without looking, and we've bounced back on to the pavement in our flight response. Once back on the pavement with the car well past, we realise we are safe, and we calm down. The left brain essentially kicks in here and tells us "I am safe now". The brain has performed its processing duty, and the potentially traumatic incident hasn't become stuck. It has been fully processed. The logical part of the brain has come in, rationalised, made sense of the fact that we are now safe, and our central nervous system has calmed down as a result. The event might have felt traumatic at the time, but the event doesn't get stuck, so effectively we have no trauma as a result, no residue of the event. We know this because, when we think back to it later, there is no emotional charge around the memory. Good. This is our brain processing threats so that they don't stay with us after the event.

Below is a picture of a fully functioning brain circuit when there is a threat, or in other words when something potentially traumatic happens. Panic and fear enter through the right brain, the feeling brain, we get to safety, then the left brain kicks in, and then everything is processed and packed away neatly with no residual "emotional charge" – no trauma. Both hemispheres of the brain are talking to each other and helping to process events to completion.

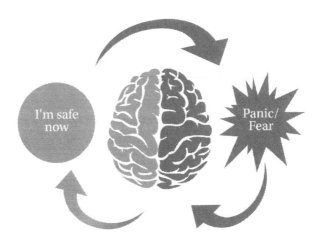

The workings of the brain during a trauma response

So, what is actually going on in our brain during a trauma response? And what causes this trauma to remain stuck inside us?

Let's think about the trauma response first.

In our brain is a small, almond-shaped thing called the amygdala. We actually have one in each hemisphere, so two in total. It's a fabulous piece of machinery. One of its roles is to detect danger, or a threat.

The amygdalae are really important. When they detect danger, or a threat, they essentially send a message to the brain that cries: "Send adrenalin through the central nervous system!" As the adrenalin courses through, we go into a state of "flight", "fight", or "freeze". We go into one or more of the three "trauma responses". Which trauma response we go into really depends on what the danger is and what our best chance of survival might be.

Think back to crossing the road. We spot the car, and the amygdala detects a threat, or danger. The amygdala sends a message to the brain saying "send adrenalin through the system!". The surge of adrenalin through the central nervous system sends us into fight or flight, and we "automatically" jump back on to the pavement. Think back to being in the middle of the road and seeing the car coming towards us! Fight or flight isn't going to work this time, so adrenalin continues to pump through the body and instead we go into "freeze". Then perhaps, if we are knocked over and are feeling totally overwhelmed and helpless, we could either remain in freeze or go into "flop" as well. More on the flop trauma response in a moment.

The left brain during a trauma response

Let's go back to the moment when we saw the car. We felt panic and fear! *Then we jumped back on to the pavement – or we froze.* Did we think about jumping back on to the pavement or freezing? No, we didn't, it just sort of happened automatically, didn't it?

The "automatic" nature of the trauma response is very important in understanding how trauma gets stuck and remains unprocessed.

At no time during either of these examples with the car did we think "I must jump back on to the pavement now", or "I must freeze now". We didn't have the time, *and it all happened at lightning speed.* If we have ever stepped out on to a road and spotted a car coming towards us, we'll realise that we didn't think at the time at all, we just jumped back – or froze. This was our clever brain and body in a sophisticated survival response, *not wasting any time on thinking at all.* Our survival response – or our trauma response – all happens in a microsecond. Even before we have felt the fear. The amygdalae are so clever at spotting danger and quick to respond with the correct brain function to get us out of that danger.

In that moment, in that moment that we didn't think, we just "acted" in order to survive. In that moment, *our thinking brain had gone "offline" because it was not needed.*

During a trauma response, we simply do not need the logical, reasoning part of our brain. The adrenalin going through our system, which is the trauma response's natural reaction to get us out of danger, is actually enough to get us out of the danger. And, possibly more importantly, if we took any time to think at all in this situation, then we simply wouldn't get out of the danger in time, and we would be much more likely to die – or be severely hurt. So we don't use the left brain; it goes offline. Thank God it goes offline; it's a matter of life or death. Clever Mother Nature. Clever body. Clever survival instincts.

Clever brain for shutting down the prefrontal cortex during a trauma response. It is the shutting down of this thinking brain that enables us to get to safety in time.

And this is all well and good, if we get out of the danger, because once the threat or the danger has passed, the left brain comes back online again. Once this happens, we can then process the event and all of the subsequent feelings that might arise. And then the event is processed. It is left in the past, where it belongs, with zero emotional charge remaining around it for us.

Trauma getting stuck – unprocessed

But let's think about when something even more horrid than avoiding a car happens to us. Imagine we had actually been hit by the car, and we'd found ourselves on the road, in pain, having been hit. We'd still be in a trauma response as we were lying in the road, because we'd still feel as though we were in danger – and the amygdala would still be signalling the brain that there was more danger. "I'm lying on the road, and I can't move", or "I might have broken something", or "I might die". We may have even more feelings coursing through us by then, and more adrenalin too.

Staying in a trauma response for longer means that our left brain is going to take a longer time to come back online. It might not even restore its services for a few days.

When it takes a while for the left brain to come back online, when we stay in the trauma response too long, then there is a very high chance that that event, and the feelings associated with it, are going to get stuck. This is because the relationship between the left and right brain has temporarily ceased.

And this "stuckness" results in unresolved trauma.

Let's think back to the Big T that we touched on in Chapter 1. Imagine we witness a terrorist attack in front of our eyes, or imagine we are physically assaulted. We cannot even begin to contemplate, let alone face, the impact that either of these horrific events might be having on our sensory system at the time. Our brain detects danger, and we interpret that danger. We might be in shock, we might be in terror, or horror – or in any of a multitude of other emotions. During the event, our left brain goes offline and those feelings do not get fully processed.

Now, it's possible that we walk away from what we have witnessed or experienced, and we manage to talk through what we have just seen or what has just happened, over the coming days or weeks, with trusted friends and family. By doing this, as time passes, the left brain begins to come back online and we can process these feelings, thereby getting through the event without too much emotional residue becoming stuck. This is the ideal outcome in terms of trauma processing, following any traumatic event. Traumatic events are unavoidable, but residual trauma can be significantly reduced if we are looked out for and given what we need following the event. Some witnesses of 9/11, for example, were able to do just this; by talking through what happened and getting the support they needed directly after the event, they managed to prevent any of the experience from becoming stuck and pestering them later down the line.

For some, however, this is not possible. We might not be able to talk it through. Maybe the experience is just all too much, too overwhelming, or too horrifying. Or maybe the trusted people required to help us process, with whom we feel safe enough to express ourselves, simply are not around – or do not exist. When we are not able to process the event at the time or in the coming days and weeks, the feelings are more likely to get stuck, and we are consequently left with unprocessed trauma.

So far we've been talking about ourselves as adults, and what happens to us as an adult when something big and scary occurs. But what about when something big and scary happens to a child? What about developmental trauma, when events aren't necessarily that "big"? Why do the feelings get stuck then?

Let's answer all of those questions now.

Developmental trauma and the brain

Just like adults, children have two amygdalae which are fully functioning from birth. Babies and children can just as easily go into a trauma response which needs to be processed, in the same way as an adult. In fact, children go into a trauma response pretty frequently, because their emotional regulation system is not yet mature enough to prevent this.

But there is one massive difference between adults and children.

When we are born, our left brain is not fully functional. In fact, our left brain does not become fully developed until we are in our early 20s.

Yet we still need to process emotional information.

From birth to three years old, we have very little left-brain function at all – which is one of the reasons why we have little to zero cognitive memories before the age of three. Very slowly, starting at the second year of life, our left brain develops, little by little, over time.

Let's think about it for a moment. Have you ever tried to have a rational and logical conversation with a three-year-old or younger child? It is simply not possible. A toddler's left brain does not have the maturity. Have you ever looked into the eyes of a baby and had a non-verbal conversation with it?

This is referred to as right-brain communication. Or feelings communication. Or intuitive communication. And this is predominantly how a baby communicates: via the right brain, the feelings brain. The left brain is simply not yet formed enough. (There is more on this in Chapter 9.)

It is actually pretty challenging to have a rational conversation with a child before they are seven years old. Even then, it has to be entirely age-appropriate or the child simply won't understand. This is because the left brain, the reasoning, logical brain, the prefrontal cortex, is not yet developed enough. But the right brain is absolutely responsive to feelings, and the brain's survival system is totally geared up for a trauma response.

So how do children process potentially traumatic events?

Answer: Adults. Caregivers. Parents. Teachers. Us. That's how.

Children need our help in a massive way. We have to be a child's left brain for them, or a variation of the left brain, at least. We have to help children regulate their emotions not only to help them process the world around them, but also in order that they are able to self-regulate later on in life.

Babies and children need our help to process emotional events and experiences.

If we don't help babies and children in the way they need it, the events, experiences, and the feelings that go with them, will remain stuck and unprocessed, and the babies and children will have unresolved trauma. This is the same both for big events and for small events.

Let's think back to the crossing the road example. This time let's imagine Little Jonny is holding his mummy's hand, and they are crossing together. But oh no, Little Jonny chooses that exact moment to let go of Mummy's hand and run across the road as the fast car is coming! What is going on for Little Jonny, as he's there in the road with a car coming towards him – panic! Fear! Mummy dashes into the road and grabs Little Jonny and hauls him back on to the pavement. Mummy is also in shock and probably panicking and scared. What does she do? She scolds Little Jonny, "What were you thinking! You are so naughty! You can't run into the road! You could have been knocked by a car!" Mummy is frightened, and she shouts at Little Jonny and scolds him, as they stand on the pavement together.

So what is going on in Little Jonny's brain? His right brain is full of shock, panic and fear, and he'll be feeling it all in his little body. He is most probably in a trauma response of flight or fight or even freeze. He needs Mummy to be the left brain, and Mummy is yelling. What happens to any child when they are yelled at? Shock! Panic! Fear! Little Jonny is experiencing more panic and fear on top of the existing panic and fear – another trauma response, more adrenalin. Mum's current left-brain support consists of: "What were you thinking! You are so naughty!" If Mum continues to scold him, Little Jonny's brain will continue to be on high alert because the situation feels so threatening.

Mum's response is not great for processing those right-brain feelings now is it? Little Jonny is left with a whole load of unprocessed shock, terror and fear, and he has adrenalin shooting through his system stressing him out further, and Mummy is yelling.

Little Jonny will be left with unresolved trauma from both the car episode and from Mum berating him. But he will probably suffer more residual trauma from Mum's yelling – as we will begin to understand more through the rest of this book.

And flop

There is another trauma response. This one is called "flop", or submit, or fawn. If our system unconsciously decides that we won't survive an incident by going into fight, flight or freeze, then we will go into a state of flop. We give up. We might even have gone into flop when we were hit by the car in the road. Little Jonny might experience the flop state if Mummy regularly scolds him and he doesn't get to express himself or stand up for himself very much.

The flop state is our way of playing dead. If an animal plays dead in the face of a predator in the wild, then there is a smaller chance it will be killed by its predator. As humans, we have this trauma response too. The "flop" trauma response is incredibly common, because so many of us had repeated traumatic experiences when we were younger. With this repetition of overwhelming childhood experiences, our system simply learned that the safest option for us was to submit, flop, acquiesce, conform, or comply.

Negative cognitions as a result of trauma

In Chapter 2, we looked at the negative self-beliefs that we can adopt as a result of trauma. We call them "negative cognitions", or "NCs". Anyone who has stuck, unprocessed trauma will have a negative cognition attached to the traumatic memory.

Let's think back to ourselves for a moment, and about when the car nearly ran us over but didn't, because of our amazing trauma flight response that got us back on to the pavement. Once we were back on the pavement again, the left brain essentially implied to us "I am safe now". Prior to that, we did not feel safe. But because the left brain kicked in with "I am safe now", there was no leftover NC, it had changed to a "positive cognition" – a "PC". "I am safe now" is a positive cognition.

But let's think about the time when we were already in the middle of the road, and we went into the "freeze" response, and we were hit by the car. As we were hit by the car, we were very much experiencing a sense of "I am in danger", or "I am not safe". And because we did get hit, the left brain didn't kick in. As well as the trauma getting stuck, the negative cognitions get stuck too. Due to the trauma not processing adequately, the NCs don't process either. Later, in trauma therapy, when looking at the car accident, when we bring up the image of that car coming towards us, we are still going to have the NC "I am in danger", or "I am unsafe" when we think about that event. Even though the event is in the past and those NCs are no longer actually true, we are still going to have the same NCs that we had at the time of the event. And they are still going to feel very, very true, until we process them with trauma therapy and give them a chance to be released.

Exactly the same thing happens when we suffer developmental trauma.

Negative cognitions and developmental trauma

Let's think back again to Little Jonny. As the car comes hurtling towards him, he has a sense of danger. So what's the NC going to be there? "I am in danger", or "I am unsafe". Both true.

On top of that, he has received the message from a yelling mum "there's something wrong with me", "it's not OK to be scared", "it's not OK to be spontaneous" and even "I am unlovable", "I am not worth it", "I am bad".

Now, Mummy is not thinking ANY of these things about Little Jonny at all. Mummy is probably glad that there wasn't an accident and that everyone is OK. *But Little Jonny doesn't know that, because Mummy hasn't said that.* All Little Jonny hears, as his terrified mum berates him, is "I am bad" – with a whole load of unprocessed scary feelings to boot.

Let's think about what Little Jonny really needed in that moment, to process this horrible experience. He needed Mummy to help him process all of these feelings. He needed Mummy to be his left brain – and more.

Let's see what that might look like in practice. We can think in terms of those 4 Ss. Little Jonny needed Mummy to haul him back on to the pavement, gather him in her arms, hug him (soothed), look him in the eye and repeat "you're safe now" (safe), "I love you" (seen / soothed / safe), "you're safe now" (safe), "I love you" (seen / soothed / safe). He needed her to do this over and over and over again (soothed) until he had calmed down (soothed); until his central nervous system had calmed down. If Mum had raised her voice, Little Jonny would have needed her to apologise and let him know that he did not deserve that (secure). Little Jonny calming down to Mum's cuddles and these words would have allowed those right-brain feelings to process, and his system would have calmed down. Little Jonny would have been soothed, and he would have felt safe. And Little Jonny would have learned "I am safe", "I am loved", "I am precious". And his system, the physiological process in his body, having been co-regulated by Mum, will be well on the path towards learning how to self-regulate later in life. And then, when Little Jonny had calmed down, perhaps then Mum could have gently explained the dangers of crossing the road, on your own, without Mummy.

What a difference 4 Ss make!

As adults, we have to be our children's left brain for them. We have to soothe them when they are in fight or flight, *because they haven't learned how to do it yet.* We need to teach them how to soothe their systems when they get hyped up – we need to *show* them how to do it.

As children, our parents are our left brain for us and our co-regulation. And this helps us learn, over time, how to self-regulate, or self-soothe, ourselves.

Thinking back to how we were parented. What sort of left-brain influence from our parents did we receive? What were those messages? Were we co-regulated? The answers to those questions are: "Probably not as much we needed". Does it make more sense now why we might have some developmental trauma?

Much of this left-brain work for parents, adults and caregivers comes in the form of soothing and providing a sense of safety. This notion of soothing and safety is so very important.

Self-soothing and self-regulation

As humans, we are constantly striving for self-regulation. Think of how the body temperature fights to stay constant. When we are hot, we sweat in order to get our body temperature down, for example. (I am writing this in a severe heatwave and I want to get into a cold bath – not because I enjoy cold baths, but because my body is urging me to help it cool down.) Or think about when we cut ourselves; the cut will heal all by itself after a few days. This self-regulation is called homeostasis. (Remember biology days? Homeostasis? I sort of do.) Our brains are just the same. Our brain is constantly striving for homeostasis too. Homeostasis = self-regulation.

This natural and instinctive striving for self-regulation begins the moment we are born.

Imagine a baby lying in its cot. It's a bit uncomfortable, so it begins to cry. Mum has been told by her mother, and by the odd parenting book too, that you must leave babies to cry otherwise they will become too needy. ("My mother always left me to cry as a baby, I was generally shoved in a pram at the bottom of the garden so that my cries didn't disturb anyone..." I've heard that one a few times, I can tell you.) The cries start gently, then they begin to elevate. The baby becomes frightened because no-one is coming, and it knows it can't look after itself. But still no-one comes. Once frightened, the baby's amygdalae send a message to the brain to pump adrenalin, and the baby goes into fight or flight. Still no-one comes. The adrenalin begins to really course through this little baby. She's in fight or flight, but she can't move because she's too little. "Flight" therefore doesn't work, and she can't "fight" because there is no-one and nothing to fight. Still no-one comes – perhaps no-one can hear, because she's stuck in a pram at the bottom of the garden. With adrenalin coursing through the system, the baby's body and brain attempts to self-regulate, but after even more adrenalin and no-one coming, the baby will most likely "flop". She falls asleep, exhausted, because her adrenal glands simply can't take any more. Mum comes over and sees baby fast asleep and says "There, clever baby has learned to self-soothe". No, I'm afraid she hasn't. She has fallen into a puddle of exhaustion after being in a trauma response for so long that her body simply couldn't cope any longer, so she has fallen asleep out of exhaustion.

Babies cannot automatically self-soothe. This is a myth. When a baby eventually falls asleep after a bout of horrific crying, they have not self-soothed themselves to sleep; they have crashed because their adrenal glands have given out, and they have given up. Babies need to be co-regulated by Mum, in order that they can self-regulate as adults (and there is more on this in Chapter 9).

Imagine if this happens to a baby often. Think of that adrenal system. It's going to spend a fair amount of time in flight or fight, freeze or flop. This baby's central nervous system is going to take a hammering. And because this is a regular experience in its life, then the "fight, flight, freeze or flop" state is going feel pretty "normal" to the baby. Wow, what a baseline, huh?

Because the baby is so young, and because at that age the brain is at the height of neuroplasticity, this baby is going to learn from infancy "my needs are not important" and "my needs do not get met". And if this type of neglect continues throughout childhood, these beliefs will become cemented (more on this in Chapter 9), and this child will grow up needing external measures in order to help soothe themselves. These external measures can look like the smoking, the drinking, the people-pleasing, the unfulfilling relationships, the workaholism, the excess shopping, the food disorders and all of the other behaviours that we discussed when we looked at the signs and symptoms of trauma.

Most babies learn to self-soothe by being shown how to do it through co-regulation with Mum.

Imagine a different scenario. Imagine Mum hears baby's cries beginning to elevate, and she sort of knows that it's no longer a little weepy cry, but that it's entering fight or flight mode. She goes to the baby, picks her up, and holds her. She rocks her in her arms and holds her close to her heartbeat. Mum tells her she is loved. Mum tells her "Mummy is here" whilst holding her. This baby's central nervous system will begin to calm down with her mum's touch and her mum's calming voice. This baby will learn "my needs are important", "when I have a need it will be met", "I am loved". This baby will come out of flight or fight with the help of her mum.

This is the baby that will learn to self-soothe when she is older. This baby will learn in that moment of desperation that she can calm down, that her system can calm down, that she is loved enough to be helped when she can't help herself, and she will learn that she is of value and that the world is a safe and loving place. And as soon as she is old enough to do her own self-soothing, she will be better placed to do it herself (provided there is no other developmental trauma of course).

This is imperative information for a baby. She will learn that she is loved. Her experience of stress will be one of "this will pass and I will be OK", "there are people there to help me".

This is the left-brain experience that the baby needs. This is how we help a baby process a difficult event.

The same applies for a young child, as we saw with Little Jonny.

If, as a baby or child, we are regularly soothed by our mum (or caregiver), then our system learns that it can calm down after a crisis, and we will consequently learn to self-soothe. If, as a baby or child, we are not soothed, we will learn that the world is not a safe and kind place, and we will have some developmental trauma.

Potentially traumatic events can be processed without residue of trauma, for both adults and children, if there is a robust enough support system in place to aid the processing of what has happened. This applies to both Big T and developmental trauma.

If there is not a good enough support system in place, and / or the traumatic events continue to occur, and / or the traumatic events are simply too overwhelming, then traumatic events and experiences will become stuck. This is true for both Big T and developmental trauma.

We need that left brain to process those feelings.

If we don't learn to self-soothe when we are children, and we have ongoing emotional abuse and neglect in our childhoods, then we will most likely turn to external coping mechanisms in order to self-soothe when we are an adult.

If we do learn to self-soothe as children – if we are shown by our caregivers how to do it – then we will not need to turn to external "stuff" when we are an adult.

If we have unmet needs when we are a child, then we will continue to search to get these needs met in adulthood – just in more "adulty" ways. For example, people-pleasing, over-use of alcohol, use of drugs, excess shopping, poor relationships with food, unfulfilling relationships and so on.

If all of our needs are met when we are a child, then we will be able to meet most of our own needs as an adult, from our own internal resources. Our brain and body will have processed difficult experiences from the past, we will have positive self-beliefs rather than negative ones, and we will have learned how to process challenging moments in our lives.

In the next chapter, we look in more detail, and with a slightly different angle, at how easily developmental trauma can occur, and also why it has stayed hidden for so long.

CHAPTER 4

How has it happened?

Instead of asking "What is wrong with this person"?
We need to be asking "What happened to this person"?

We have some of the answers to how trauma can happen from Chapters 1 to 3. Our system is primed to unconsciously be on the lookout for threats, and very often we do not have the opportunity to process events either because they are too soon – we are too young – or they are simply too much for us to process at the time.

We know by now that trauma is the result of feelings, thoughts and fragments from an event or experience, that we couldn't process at the time, that have therefore become stuck and unprocessed in our minds and our bodies.

We have also looked at a few ways in which we could have held on to some trauma ourselves, either from the horrible things that might have happened to us, and / or the lack of the 4 Ss in our childhood, or a combination of both.

This chapter looks in a bit more detail – with the help of some really easy to visualise diagrams – at what is going on between our parents and us as children, that prevents these 4 Ss from being delivered to us, and what happens to us as a result.

This is important in our understanding about how we have come to be the way we are. And we will also realise how easy it was for our parents to leave us with unhealed wounds, without them even knowing that it was happening.

It is not our fault

For many years, people suffering with any of the trauma symptoms – anxiety, depression, self-harm, addictions, eating disorders, or other trauma symptoms that we explored in the previous chapters – were thought to have something wrong with them. And sadly, this assumption continues today. "What is wrong with this person?" is a question that is asked so many times. And as if that's not bad enough, very often the person who is suffering will also carry a belief "there is something wrong with me as a person".

What we really need to be asking, however, is "What happened to this person?".

Because something did. Or some things did. And it is these things that happened – or things that didn't happen – and our experience of that, which is stuck in our systems, making us feel how we feel.

Let's take a look.

Emotional attunement

I introduced the concept of emotional attument in Chapter 1. We will further explore its importance here. As I mentioned, emotional attunement is an ability to sense another's feelings and mood states, and thus their needs. It becomes a bond between a parent (or caregiver) and a child, provided by the parent (or caregiver), in order that the child grows up with minimal developmental trauma.

In order for a child to grow up and become a fully functioning, emotionally whole adult, they need a parent who is emotionally attuned to them enough of the time. This is preferably both parents, but just having one parent connected to us in this way is a good start.

This unconditional, emotional attunement, provided by our parent whilst we are growing up, produces a deep connection from our parent to us. This sense of connection provided by our parent allows us to feel safe, loved, understood, respected, and treasured (Safe, Seen, Soothed and Secure) for exactly who we are, and how we are, at any given moment. In our ideal world, our parent fulfils all of these needs, which is exactly what we require to take place in order that we can mature in a healthy and whole way.

A child requires their emotional needs to be met on every level, enough of the time.

Let's look at this notion of emotional attunement in pictures.

Jim Knipe, a brilliant EMDR therapist and teacher, originally came up with the idea of these diagrams. I have borrowed them from him.

The Ideal Parent-Child Connection

Diagram 1:

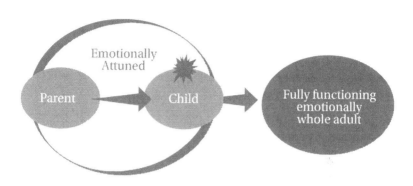

If we look at Diagram 1, we can see the parent and the child tucked comfortably inside a bubble. This bubble signifies the parent's emotional attunement. It's lovely. It is whole, it is holding, and it is complete.

Within that bubble, you might notice an arrow connecting the parent and the child; the arrow is coming from the parent, towards the child. Imagine we are that child. This arrow shows us that the parent is forging a connection with us. All we need, as this child, is to be our glorious, messy and authentic self. The spiky blob represents our glorious child-like messiness. With our parent's unconditional holding, as this child we can fully experience what it is like to be human. We can safely express all of the emotions that human beings feel on the entire feelings spectrum. And we will know that this parent is emotionally available for us, as and when needed.

You might notice the next arrow, outside the big bubble, that points to the child as an adult. With the gift of unconditional, emotional attunement from the parent during childhood, this child can grow into a fully functioning, emotionally whole adult, with very little – if any – unresolved emotional trauma.

Unfortunately, Diagram 1. demonstrates an ideal scenario and, in reality, it is quite rare to have had this level of emotional attunement from our parents. What generally happens is this:

What generally happens

Diagram 2:

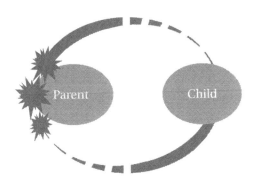

Diagram 2 does not have the lovely bubble of emotional attunement. Instead, it has some patchy lines connecting the parent to the child.

Diagram 2 is demonstrating that the parent's emotional attunement is patchy. It might be there at times, for sure, but perhaps not to the degree that the child in this diagram really needs it to be. This is pretty common for most of us, this is what generally happens to us. We will find out what happens as a result of this throughout the rest of the chapter.

Do you notice those big, black, spiky blobs around the parent in Diagram 2? These black, spiky blobs represent the parent's unresolved trauma from the past. They have carried their own unresolved trauma from the past into their role as a parent, resulting in us as a child not receiving the level of emotional attunement that we really needed.

We can – and should – use these diagrams with either Dad or Mum in the box because both Mum and Dad will have their own trauma, and it might be the same or different from each other. I have put the word "parent" in just to show as an example that this can apply to either parent.

We can see, from Diagram 2, that the parent has their own trauma that they have not yet resolved. This might be Big T, it might be developmental trauma, it might be generational trauma or societal trauma (more on this in the next chapter), and it might be a mixture of all of the above. Either way, it is all unresolved, and it is shaping how the parent functions, while preventing the parent from being able to be, or feel, unconditionally attuned to their child.

The unresolved trauma that our parents bring into the relationship with us as children significantly impacts their ability to connect with us in the way that we need it.

In order for a parent to be emotionally attuned to their child, they need to be emotionally attuned to themselves. To be emotionally attuned to themselves, they need to have resolved an enormous amount of their own backstory – their own trauma.

Let's have a look at the next diagram. Here we can begin to see what happens to a child in the absence of an emotionally attuned parent.

Diagram 3:

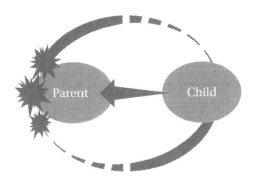

Do you notice, in Diagram 3, how the arrow is now going in the opposite direction? In the first diagram, in the ideal parent-child connection, the arrow was coming from the parent and pointing towards the child. This is what we want to be happening. But in this picture, in Diagram 3, where the parent has their own unresolved trauma and is not able to be emotionally attuned enough of the time, *the arrow is facing towards the parent, originating from the child.*

And this is key.

Because, if our parent has unresolved past material and they are not able to make a solid enough connection with us as a child, enough of the time, *then we as the child have to work to forge that connection with our parent.*

We need to feel connected

As children, we NEED to feel connected with a parent. If that connection isn't being forged by a parent to us, then we ourselves take care of forging that connection with our parent. And we do this unconsciously. It is a survival mechanism. We do this because the notion of not being connected to our parent is, on an unconscious level, way too much for us even to contemplate as a child, let alone tolerate.

We need to feel connected to our parents in order that we feel able to survive.

In order for us to forge that connection with our parent, as children, we quickly work out what our parent can and cannot tolerate, or will and will not tolerate, and we change ourselves accordingly, in order that we are "approved of" (i.e. "loved") by our parent.

> *"Children choose connection over authenticity"*
> – Gabor Maté

As Gabor Maté, a trauma writer, teacher and coach, who brought the link between addiction and trauma to the mainstream, so perfectly states: "Children choose connection over authenticity."

It is all about survival.

In order to survive and feel connected to our parents, as children we work out which feeling states and behaviours our parents do not "allow" (or cannot tolerate), and we change ourselves accordingly. We do this even if it goes against our true nature, or our true self. Remember, it is all about survival, and we do it unconsciously.

As children, we know, on an instinctive level, that we need food, shelter, clothing, a home, and a feeling of belonging and acceptance. But we are not developed enough yet to work out how to keep that sense of survival going without keeping Mum and Dad happy; we are simply too young. We do not yet have a fully-functioning pre-frontal cortex (left-brain), and our limbic system (right-brain) is still in charge; we are not mature enough yet to be able to state our truths, especially if they are in discord with those of our parents. What we do know though, is that we need Mum and Dad to be happy in order for the family unit to function. And we unconsciously decide to do whatever it takes to make sure that this happens.

Therefore, in order that we can feel the sense of belonging, acceptance and unity that we so crave, we change ourselves to fit in with what our parent will accept and tolerate.

Shutting off and shutting down

You might be wondering what we do with our real stuff, what we do with those authentic parts of us that we know our parent cannot tolerate.

I'll tell you. It's clever, but it is sad. We unconsciously shut down those parts of ourselves that Mum or Dad can't handle. Yup, we'll shut them right off, and we'll shut them right down. We shut down and shut off any parts of us that we have either sensed, or know, are not welcome in the family unit. These might be feelings – they might be behaviours. Whichever they are, we shut them down.

Diagram 4:

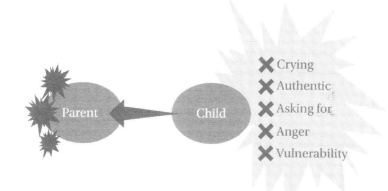

We can see from Diagram 4 that this child has shut down their anger, their sadness and their tears, they have stopped asking for help, and they have shut down their vulnerability; they have shut down many of their authentic human parts.

The child in this diagram has worked out, cleverly and unconsciously, that, in order to be part of the family system and to feel connected to their parents, they must not show any of their feelings or behaviours that the parents cannot tolerate. This probably means that the parent has either overtly (obviously and vocally) or covertly (subtly hinted at) rejected these feelings or behaviours. For us to experience those feelings of rejection and lack of connection again by keeping those parts of us in plain sight, is simply too much for us to tolerate. So we shut it all down.

Meeting our parents' needs

By doing this, by shutting down parts of ourselves in order to feel connected to our parents, we are actually meeting our parents' needs.

And yup, that's completely the wrong way around. Because, of course, the parent should be meeting the child's needs.

Our parents, and their parents before them, might not have had any conscious awareness of the importance of emotional attunement. And as a result of this, we have been traumatised as children, just like our parents before us.

And if we are not aware of it – we will be doing the same, or similar, to our children, without even realising that it is happening.

Agreements that we make

Another notion that Jim Knipe has given voice to is that when we change ourselves, in order to fit in with our parents, we are unconsciously making agreements with ourselves around how to react and respond as children.

These might look like some of the following:

I agree to be perfect
I agree to be quiet
I agree to be super clean

I agree to wear what I am told even if I hate it
I agree to be friends with my parents' friends' children
I agree to be the good one whilst my disabled sibling takes up all the space
I agree to have friends approved of by my mum
I agree to not get angry
I agree to not cry
I agree to not have an opinion; it is my mum's way or the highway
I agree that my parents choose my study path, not me
I agree that I am "overemotional" if I show too much emotion
I agree to look after my mum because she is sad
I agree to look after my dad because he is sad
I agree to be seen and not heard
And the list goes on...

As we are reading this, perhaps we can think about what agreements we personally made, when we were little, in order to ensure we remained connected with our parents – in order that we could survive. We will have made some. I know I did.

When we are a child, of course we don't sit down and say those things to ourselves, but if we take a moment to sit with our inner system now, we can feel that our psyche did make agreements, changing our authentic selves, in order to fit in with what our parents expected of us.

And when we change parts of ourselves and make these agreements, as children, we are seeking to meet Mum and Dad's needs, instead of having Mum and Dad meet our needs.

Just take a moment and have another look at the list above; you will notice that we can insert the phrase "to fulfil Mum / Dad's need" with every single statement, with every agreement that we made.

We spend much of our childhoods fulfilling our parents' needs – rather than what is supposed to happen in a parent-child relationship, which is, of course, that the parent should fulfil the child's needs. Sadly, this leaves us with developmental deficits, as mentioned in the prior chapters, which leads to us seeking to get those child needs met right on through our adult life. This is one of the main reasons adult relationships can be so challenging; we are still seeking to have our childhood needs met through our partners, and our partners don't really fit the role that our parents should have had – nor should they.

So here we are, with a whole lot of parts of ourselves shut off, or shut down. So how do we function? Good question. Let's take a look.

The apparently normal part / person

Despite so many of our needs and our parts being shut down, we still need to function as children. We want to be part of the family unit, and we want to be part of life. We have sacrificed our authenticity, but we are still alive.

Jim Knipe speaks to this brilliantly. He talks about how we then go on to develop an "apparently normal person" (ANP for short). And this is what we do – in order to survive.

Let's look at Diagram 5.

Diagram 5:

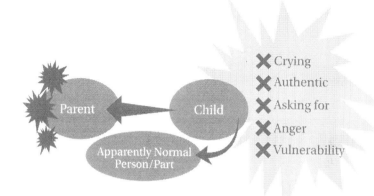

This apparently normal person / part (ANP) is fantastic. It carries on with life. The ANP ensures that we do school, have friends, have play dates, find hobbies. And it continues into adulthood, taking us through university, into jobs, marriages, and having children. It helps us to do whatever we choose and are capable of. We know how to "do" life on the outside, so we do it. We see our parents doing it, we see our friends doing it, so we do it too. We operate in our lives predominantly from the ANP, the apparently normal person (or part).

But I wonder what is really going on for us, on the inside, with all of those shut off and shut down parts of ourselves. What happens to them?

Emotions are energy

All of the parts of ourselves that we have to shut down, in order that we can forge an attachment with our parent, have feelings or emotions shut down with them – unprocessed feelings and emotions. These emotions are either left over from unprocessed memories and events or experiences themselves, or from just having to shut those feelings down. Or through lack of the 4 Ss. Or as a result of all of the above.

If we have shut down and shut off parts of ourselves from our real self, then we are in trouble, because we have a whole host of unprocessed emotions brewing inside us.

We think we've turned these feelings off forever. We think that by shoving them under the carpet that they will stay sweetly silent for us.

But feelings can't actually be turned off. We can put a lid on them and have them *feel* like they're turned off, but actually they are still simmering inside us.

Emotion is derived from the Latin "emotere" which means "energy in motion". E-motion.

Feelings are energy. They are energy with a message. Feelings propel us towards something in their message – or rather their energy does.

If we don't process our feelings, but we just pack them away, *these feelings do not actually go away.*

So what happens to them? What happens to us when we have packed away so much of our authentic self in order that our parent approves of us?

Let's take a look.

Defences

Diagram 6:

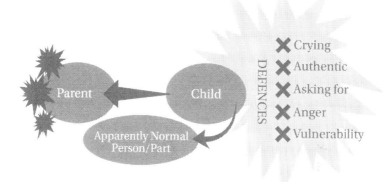

Have a look at Diagram 6. In order to keep those feelings tucked away, we need to build a line of defences.

And these defences also keep the ANP from being busted for not really being whole or authentic.

Remember, all of the feelings continue to fire off, even though we think we've buried them. That's why they are in a spiky shape rather than a smooth circle. It's because they're still firing inside us.

Defences, however, stop those feelings from suddenly bubbling up and exploding.

Defences keep our ANP in place.

Defences stop people from seeing the real us – the hidden parts of us – the part of us that we are ashamed of because our parents didn't approve of them.

Defences are our saving grace to keep us functioning.

Defences become our friends.

Defences help us to feel soothed and safe.

We need our defences desperately, because the last thing we want is for those disallowed feelings or unmet needs to suddenly come to the surface. Good God, we don't want people thinking we're angry, or overemotional, or too needy, do we? If it was not allowed when we were a child, then our system is firmly of the belief that these emotions are not acceptable. And, people know us as the ANP! We just get on with things! We cope so well! Our day-to-day making a living might even rely on our ANP. As an adult, our own children and our own family unit might rely on our ANP. If that ANP gets busted, we might feel like our entire life will be swept away. It just might feel too overwhelming to contemplate. We might fear abandonment or rejection, or we might fear the shame of being found out, if the real us were to be revealed.

Defences include:

Addictions, anxiety, depression, people-pleasing, caretaking, inability to say no, narcissism, bullying, feeling like a victim, co-dependency, excessive shopping, excessive eating, eating disorders, disordered eating, restricted eating, criminal activity, workaholism, always needing to be busy, inability to stop and do nothing, reaching for anything external to make us feel better, obsession with material things, a constant need for "more". Anything to stop those feelings from coming up and busting our ANP.

Defences are our methods of self-protection.

Do you recognise those defences from Chapter 2?

They are exactly the same list as the signs and symptoms of unresolved trauma.

Our defences, our methods of self-protection, our ways of coping to make sure that our authentic self is never seen, are all signs that we have unresolved trauma.

All of the defence behaviours that we partake in to protect the "apparently normal person" that we have become, with so much of our authentic self hidden, are at worst dysfunctional – or at best, self-defeating.

But they are also all forms of self-protection. They are protecting us from having to feel all of those feelings we shut down years ago. They are protecting us from feeling and remembering all of the memories of those horrid things that happened. All the grief, panic and terror around the loving, accepting things that didn't happen, and the authentic parts of ourselves that were completely disallowed whilst we were developing our neural wiring – they are all being protected by these behaviours. We might even find that we are completely out of touch with these deep feelings. Our defences have been in place for so long that we don't even realise these buried emotions are inside us.

Our defences are literally helping us to survive. They were formed out of a need for survival, and they remain with us out of a need for survival. It is all about survival.

Intent versus how it is received

It is really important here – and always – to talk about the notion of "intent" on the part of the parent.

You might remember Chapter 3, when Mum pulled Little Jonny back on to the pavement, terrified, and probably in traumatic reaction herself. She scolded Little Jonny, because she was so scared and panicky herself. Little Jonny took on the negative beliefs along the vein of "I am bad", "I am not loved by Mummy", "it's all my fault", "I am worthless". Now of course, Mummy is not thinking these things at all, but that is neither here nor there, because Little Jonny believes that about himself based on what is happening, and because Mummy is scolding him for nearly being run over. Mum did not intend that Little Jonny make those decisions about himself, but based on Mum's behaviour and words, Little Jonny takes on those beliefs.

Rosie, 42, came to me with disordered eating and struggling

to find a romantic partner. She had toyed with anorexia and bulimia when she was younger, but mostly now overate in the evenings when she was alone. She was sent to boarding school when she was eight. She said she really enjoyed boarding school, she loved the fun, she loved being with so many other children her age, and she loved the weekend activities. Really fun she said. She told me she had cried for the first two weeks of term for the first year, but that she had got over that with the help of a very stern matron and the fact that they weren't allowed to make phone calls home, so it made it easier to forget. I asked her if she felt abandoned those tearful first few weeks. Her response was "I wasn't abandoned, all my friends' parents' sent their children to boarding school, we lived in the country and the best schools were really far away. Everyone did it". I smiled internally. How many times have I heard this one before? "Yes, of course," I replied, "I'm not suggesting your parents intentionally abandoned you at all."

And I asked her: "But did you *feel* abandoned?"

On hearing my question, Rosie welled up, and I could feel the pain and sadness in the room. She looked at me with her now damp eyes and heaviness in her chest, and she said "Oh my God, yes I did. I felt abandoned, lost, and very alone".

I can't tell you the number of times I have heard this story, Rosie is not alone. When she and I started the work, one of the first "events" that she went back to was being dropped off at boarding school for the first time, and her negative belief was very firmly "I am abandoned" because, when she dug deep, that is exactly how she felt. We processed it. She cried and cried and cried. She cried all of those feelings that she hadn't been allowed to cry out at the time. She processed the matron who had told her to "Get up now and dry your eyes" – very kindly – every morning that she had woken, sobbing with homesickness. At the time, due to matron needing to get everyone out of bed, she had had to stuff the rest of her tears back down before getting dressed and heading off to breakfast, where she had had to eat her cereal and toast regardless of her lack of appetite. She found that the food helped with how sad she felt, and she later went on to use food as a form of comfort any time things became too much. We worked together for a few months, going back in time to other unprocessed memories, desensitising the feelings that Rosie had blocked off from her childhood, her brain naturally rewiring in the process. At the end, she was no longer held back in life by past events. She no longer comfort eats in the evenings, or any time for that matter, and she has a much calmer outlook on life.

We do need to understand how the actions, and inactions, of our parents and other adult caregivers in our childhoods affected us. And by the same token, we need to understand how our actions and inactions affect our children.

However, it is also really important to understand that none of this has been consciously intended. Rosie's parents certainly did not intend to traumatise her by sending her away to school. The matron certainly did not intend to traumatise Rosie by telling her to stop crying.

Every mother and father strives to do the absolute best for their child. Which parent doesn't? Only about 1% of my clients had parents who intentionally harmed them. Some parents might have been too conditioned or too selfish to give much thought to how they raised their children emotionally, sure, but only around 1% of parents intentionally harmed their children. Yet remember, 99% of people I see have developmental trauma. Most parents honestly believe that whatever modality they choose as their parenting style is absolutely the best that there is out there and absolutely the best for their child. None of this is intended by the parents.

Unfortunately, intent is not enough when it comes to trauma.

And we might hit points in our healing journey where we feel livid beyond measure around what happened. And we need to face those feelings head-on, and process them, in order that we can come through it.

Shame

There is another reason why there is so much trauma, and why it has stayed hidden, and why it continues to plague people, and this is such a big one I have given it its own chapter. And this reason is shame.

We have to wait for Chapter 6 to learn about shame though, because the next chapter is a very, very important one and explains, in more depth, how trauma has stayed hidden for so long.

CHAPTER 5

Why does our trauma stay hidden?

"For twenty years I observed people denying their childhood traumas, idealizing their parents and resisting the truth about their childhood by any means."

– Alice Miller

Alice Miller was a psychoanalyst, and she wrote the above quote in 1985, at the age of 62. This was almost 35 years ago, and even then she had been observing people, as part of her work, for 20 years. Other prominent mental health professionals, including Carl Jung, who died in 1961 aged 85, also talked about how humans will do anything, no matter how absurd, to avoid looking at their own souls. For decades, there have been serious healthcare professionals in the Western world fully aware that we deny our childhood trauma – and the process of talking about it – yet many of us are still struggling to understand its impact, both on our own lives and on the lives of our children.

Why is this? Why is there this hidden trauma epidemic that relatively few people understand is happening?

Defences work – until they don't

We already know that unresolved trauma hurts. And we have already learned that we can unconsciously put a whole range of defences in place to protect our hurt from being realised and / or felt.

But one of the reasons that our unresolved trauma stays hidden is because defences are brilliant, and they work. Sometimes we even really love them. We love the feeling of that first sip of alcohol entering our body. We love the feeling of those first drags of a cigarette. We love our eating disorder. We feel safe in our depression – that might sound odd, but we often do. Similarly with our anxiety – we are so used to it, it does become a bit of a friend. We love the high of over-shopping, because it makes us feel good, and perhaps we get a thrill from not quite being able to afford it (or from being able to). We love overworking, because it makes us feel productive, worthy and good enough. We love over-exercising, because we love those endorphins, and the feeling of being fit and toned, and we feel safe that we are keeping fit and have a purpose.

We love all of our defences because we like the feeling of soothing and safety that they bring.

But there are other reasons why our trauma can stay hidden, and this chapter will look at them too. We will look at the role of the normalisation of trauma within family systems and the normalisation of trauma within societies. We will also look at generational trauma and how unresolved trauma is passed down the generations, with many of us not even realising that this even occurs.

Those who already seek help for their trauma

For some people of course, their trauma does not stay hidden. Many, many people have trauma therapy every day, and there are thousands of trauma therapists all over the world doing amazing work all day, every day.

But very often, the people who are deciding that enough is enough and that they want - or have to - examine their inner world, are the ones who have suffered the most.

For the people who have suffered the most, their emotional discomfort becomes too much, and they know something has to change. Perhaps their trauma adaptations or defences have ceased to work so well for them. Perhaps their relationships are suffering because of their drinking, gambling or raging, or their body weight has become too low with anorexia. Perhaps their binge eating is damaging their oesophagus, their intestines and bowel; perhaps their anxiety is causing them to stay at home, too worried about leaving the house.

Or perhaps their triggers are negatively affecting their life to such a degree that lots of things start going badly wrong for them.

Many people who have a psychiatrically recognised mental ill health problem might come forward for help because life just isn't sustainable for them with their maladaptive behaviours, anymore. Of course, many people who suffer to this level do not come forward for help, and this is a tragedy of the highest proportion.

Some people only seek help for trauma when they have obvious signs of PTSD. They know something horrific happened to them, and they remain haunted by nightmares, flashbacks, panic attacks, avoidance of reminders, overwhelming feelings, mood swings, and obvious changes of behaviour that have come about since the event itself. We are now much more conscious around the concept of PTSD than we used to be, and this is great.

Another thing that can cause us to seek help, is that our past, unresolved traumas can suddenly be triggered to the point of not being able to be ignored. This can happen if there is another big traumatic event, for example a divorce, the death of someone close, a major job and security loss – or a global pandemic. Traumatic incidents in our adult lives can trigger past, unresolved trauma that we did not even know we were carrying.

And who are those who don't seek help?

But there are many people too, who absolutely do not consider asking for help. Perhaps our emotional despair is not overbearing or in the forefront of our awareness. Perhaps our dysfunctional behaviours don't really bother us too much. Perhaps our triggered behaviour is more or less accepted by us, and by those around us, in both our family system and in society. Perhaps we do not realise that help is available to enable us to feel *even better* in our lives than we already do.

And this is another thing that keeps people traumatised. Not feeling the need to change, not feeling as though it is societally acceptable to admit we need help, or simply accepting "this is my lot" and struggling on. So we keep our trauma hidden.

Inherited behaviours

So much of the pain we are carrying simply is not ours.

Much of the time, we don't even realise that we are acting out on our unresolved trauma, acting out on our wounds. Sometimes this is because the trauma adaptations and behaviours themselves are inherited from our parents.

When we are young, we often mirror the behaviour of our parents.

If we have parents who are people-pleasers, we might well become a people-pleaser ourselves, because we have witnessed our parents (or parent) behaving like that, and we think that this behaviour is correct and normal.

If we have parents who shame us, we will probably shame our children, because we believe that it is in the best interests of our children to do so – it was done to us and we're OK, so we'll do it to our children.

If we had parents who struggled around earning or spending money, we might well adopt this too.

If we are raised in a family that insists on keeping secrets within the family, we might carry this notion into our family system when we have our own children. We might retain the belief that it's not OK to air one's dirty laundry in public, or admit that beneath our family veneer things are less than rosy.

If we have a family that regularly drinks alcohol, then we will probably learn that not only is this OK, but that it is also "part of life". Many people who do put down alcohol, and enter into recovery, are then told by their family members "poor you, not being able to drink".

If we were smacked as a child, we might think that it is OK to smack our children.

Inherited belief systems

If we think back to Chapter 4, we will remember how our parents, because of their own unresolved trauma, very often could not tolerate our authentic self. We had to change ourselves accordingly, in order to meet the needs of our parents, because we were too young to know any different. That sense of connection with the unit is of the utmost importance to us when we are little, over and above our authenticity.

But if our parents cannot tolerate the real us, how on earth are we going to think that anyone else might tolerate the real us? We adopt our parents' belief systems, as our own, in order to feel safe and connected. And because this occurs whilst our neural pathways are forming, it feels as though these belief systems belong to our authentic self too.

If our family does not tolerate anger, for example, we might develop a belief system that implies anger is "bad". We will therefore continue suppressing our anger in later life, and we will think that anger is unacceptable because that is what we have learned. We might become physically ill as a result of all that repressed emotion inside us, or we might turn into a "rager", unable to regulate our anger.

If we had a mother or father who simply didn't feel good enough about themselves, then we will quite possibly feel not good enough about ourselves too. We have literally adopted our parents' beliefs towards themselves.

If we had parents who told us the world was a dangerous place and that life is hard, then we will most likely develop a belief system that holds "I am not safe" and / or "life is supposed to be hard".

If we were taught as youngsters "boys don't cry", and we never saw our dad cry, then we are both told and shown that we don't cry if we are a boy. We most probably won't cry as adult men in that case, and we might even feel "weak" if we do. And we might feel weak if we admit to, or show, a mere glimmer of vulnerability.

If we are brought up in a family where women are regarded as second-class citizens, then, as women, we might feel second class to men as we enter into our adult lives.

If we are raised in a family where feelings and emotions are not celebrated, or if we are told outright that feelings are not important in life, then we will probably tuck our own emotions away for most of our lives too.

If we had a family who did not openly grieve losses, then we will most probably tuck away our own, unprocessed grief as well.

And so it goes on.

When these messages come from our parents, during our childhood, then we will most probably learn that these messages are absolutely true, and we will adopt them as our own behaviours and beliefs too.

Because when we're little, our mum and dad are gods. They are literally our god. What they say goes. How they behave goes. We believe it all. Because they feel like God. Our god. (There is another reason too, and that will be explained in the next chapter, Chapter 6.)

So, if Mum and Dad have their own unresolved trauma, and their own trauma adaptations, *we are going to adopt many of them.* Or, we might completely rebel and do the polar opposite of what our parents did to us – that's quite common too.

Some parents will overcompensate with their children, for what they did not receive, without even realising they are doing it.

When Bella, at the age of 35, had her first child, she wouldn't let her baby out of her sight for the first nine months of her baby's life. She wouldn't let a grandparent or friend take the sleeping baby out for a walk and she barely slept at night in case the baby woke to find she wasn't right there. She kept her baby strapped to her front all day, for fear that if she allowed her baby to sleep alone, even for a moment, that the baby would feel abandoned and alone. She did all of this despite feeling exhausted, sleep-deprived and depleted. Bella only realised, four years later, when she started trauma therapy, that she had huge abandonment trauma from her childhood, and that she was unconsciously overcompensating for this with her new baby, terrified her new baby might feel abandoned if she couldn't see Mum all of the time. Bella's trauma was predominantly an attachment rupture with her mother, and she was able to heal this in the sessions.

Another way that this overcompensating can play out is by the parent unconsciously knowing, deep inside, that they have a deep feeling of rejection, and they consequently crave this attention from their children. This, of course, is completely the wrong way around and desperately unhealthy for children to experience.

But the reasons we do all of this are largely out of our control. When we are viewing our parents akin to God, especially in the years before we are seven, eight or nine years old (more on this in Chapter 9), our neural networks are wiring to form our internal view of ourselves, of others, and of the world. During this time, our prefrontal cortex is not yet developed enough to make our own rational judgement and meaning about everything that is going on around us. So we take on the belief systems of our parents, and they become predominantly wired in our brain, even if they don't feel quite right to us.

And then we develop survival strategies to help us compensate for that sense of "this doesn't feel quite right". And these survival strategies become our defences.

We are most probably going to pass our parents' beliefs down to our children too, because that's what happened to us, and that is our "normal". And we justify it by thinking to ourselves that we can work, we can sleep, we can play, we can get married, we can have children – so what could have possibly been wrong with the way in which we were brought up? That's what we think; that's what we rationalise. That is a way of us reconciling the conflict inside us. And all of this contributes to the normalisation of trauma, and the normalisation of trauma adaptations.

Normalisation of trauma within families

All of these inherited belief systems within families will feel very "normal" to the developing child. And as the child gets older, they will still feel pretty normal.

The behaviours are all passed on, because they have become normalised within the family system and they are what we know.

We might even feel guilty if we don't partake in our parents' trauma responses. So many young people feel guilty for not being perfectionists, not being workaholics, or not being anorexics like one of their parents. They then feel ashamed of not being good enough. They are still regarding the parent's traumatic symptoms as "how we are supposed to be". Children as young as eight are being admitted to hospital with restricted eating and often comment how their other family members don't eat enough either. An adult from a childhood family with parents raised on wartime rations might feel guilty about throwing away food, or even spending money.

Even physical abuse can be normalised. Imagine a child brought up in a household where it's "normal" to smack children. Each time this child receives a smack, or sees a sibling receive a smack, the child is going to feel scared. The brain will detect danger, and the child's brain will automatically organise a trauma response in an unconscious fraction of a second – fight, flight, freeze or, if it happens a lot over time, flop. And this trauma response can become normalised too, as we will see from Laila now.

Laila was regularly smacked as a child. I asked, one session, what it was like for her being smacked, and her first response was "I deserved it". As we started to do the trauma work, and Laila started to process the smacking events, the feelings that had been stuck there emerged, and she pretty quickly realised that every time she had been smacked, she had either been in fight, flight, freeze or flop as it was happening – and as she anticipated it happening too. What she also noticed was that the flop response was the most prevalent; she had given up. The flop response had sadly taken root for Laila, and these feelings of helplessness, hopelessness and powerlessness that she experienced around the smacking had continued throughout her adult life. It took a fair few sessions, and a lot of psycho-education (rather like the information in this book), for her to break through this feeling of flop. But she persevered until her child psyche felt strong, in control, and able to stand up to her mum and dad in those memories of being smacked. It was really brave, and it was hard work on her part, allowing her neural networks to rewire and allow self-love to come in and to heal her, but it happened. She got there.

Generally, of course, with a parent who considers smacking

to be a regular enough form of punishment, there is going to be an absence of many more of the 4 Ss for the child, so of course we take this into consideration, and Laila was in a state of "flop" for a lot of her childhood – powerless, helpless and hopeless. Even though she developed an eating disorder and self-harmed as a result, she didn't know that inherited belief systems and unresolved trauma, as a result of overt abuse, were contributing to why she played with food and cut herself. She does now. Those feelings of helpless, hopeless and powerlessness no longer exist for her. She feels strong, powerful and good enough, and she is no longer controlled by her eating disorder.

Any child spending the majority of their developmental years in a state of flop will enter their adult lives feeling powerless, helpless and hopeless, unable to take control of their lives, and often still with disordered eating, social anxiety, and relationship difficulties.

But the other trauma responses from childhood also continue into adulthood too.

Living with a central nervous system on high alert has become our normal. And all of our dysfunctional behaviours – our trauma responses – have been normalised within the family system.

Normalisation of trauma within society

If we think back to Chapter 2, and some of the less well-known symptoms of trauma, we can perhaps understand a little more how this epidemic has been hidden for so long. Some of these signs and symptoms of trauma are not only socially accepted, but they are also often encouraged. Yet they are all trauma responses!

How many successful businessmen need a personal assistant who is a perfectionist, or who is willing to give up their own life for their boss 24/7, for example? How many businesses and companies aspire to their employees overachieving? How many companies still encourage their employees to work silly, long hours, negatively affecting their health? Many, many, many, many still do. Children in schools are also encouraged to "overachieve" in order that they can adequately join the workforce later, and the competition for school places – along with the standards that need to be reached in order to attain this – is becoming greater each year, certainly in the UK.

Perfectionism, overachieving and working ourselves to the bone are all trauma responses. And they are largely normalised in our society.

Let's look, for a moment, at the societal attitude to restricting food. Food restriction is a trauma response, yet large fashion designers still put unhealthily thin models on their catwalks. However much we hope it will change – and it is beginning to change slowly – there still exists a glory in being thin. Petra, a client in her 20s, found it almost impossible to agree that for a seven-year-old being skinny was not important, because she has witnessed, in her adult life, that there still exists a correlation between being thin and achieving success or being accepted. This made it much harder for her younger self to process an experience of being told she was fat.

People-pleasing, powering through, not taking holidays, prioritising career over personality, being a yes-person, workaholism, overscheduling, or functioning on a few hours' sleep – these are all signs and symptoms that we have trauma. They are all trauma responses. They are all protective defence layers that we have unconsciously put in place in order to avoid how we really feel underneath. And they have been normalised by society.

How many people do you know who just say, when you ask how they are: "I'm so busy!" The "busyness" culture is also a normalised trauma response.

Societal norms that are actually trauma responses will naturally contribute to a trauma epidemic.

Cultural trauma norms

Some cultural norms, the norms that are ingrained in a society's culture, despite being traumatic for any human psyche, are also normalised.

Abdel, from Lebanon, came for trauma healing and, as we were taking a trauma history, I asked him if he had had any exposure to war zones as part of the generalised trauma history taking. His response was "Yes of course, I was born with bombs dropping all around me, but that's not traumatic for me, that is just how it was and it was our normal". Abdel's central nervous system baseline was set so high, due to the number of times he had gone into flight or fight as a baby, that he didn't even consider a bomb going off as being traumatic anymore.

Khalid, during his trauma history, told me that his father had smacked him a lot when he was younger. He continued by saying "But it's a cultural thing in India, we were all smacked". This normalisation of smacking had caused him to bury the pain of being smacked very, very deep indeed.

Olivia, brought up in the UK and sent to boarding school at eight years old, suffering from abandonment trauma, found the notion of feeling abandoned very difficult to come to terms with because being sent to boarding school was such a "normal" thing to happen in the UK if you had the money for it and you lived in an area of the country that was far away from good schools.

Cultural norms that are actually trauma responses will naturally contribute to a trauma epidemic. These norms will naturally encourage us to bury our emotional pain, and we won't even realise that we are hurting.

Another thing we can consider is that of globalisation. Despite its merits, for many people there can be trauma associated with leaving their place of birth and entering into a new society, and a new culture, in a new country. Perhaps they will be regarded as second-class citizens, or their qualifications will not be recognised in the new country, and they are powerless to change it. This level of societal trauma is rife – as I'm sure we all know – and has been going on for a very long time.

Love and loyalty

Another way of looking at all of this, and something we also might consider, is that deep down we really do love our parents and our grandparents. We feel a tremendous sense of loyalty to them, and to how they did things, and we do not wish to disrespect this. Of course, many of the behaviours and beliefs that we have inherited will also be serving us very well. Sometimes it might feel hard for us to be able to tell the difference between what works for us and what doesn't, because our desire to remain loyal to the family or societal system feels very entrenched.

Very often this sense of loyalty remains strong even when our inherited belief systems and behaviours are harmful for us, or when they keep us stuck.

And both of these points can further serve to prevent us from realising our truth, keeping us stuck in our conditioning and acting out in ways that do not serve us.

Generational trauma

Generational trauma is unresolved trauma passed down through the generations. And it happens. It happens a lot.

Intergenerational trauma is the trauma passed down from our parents and grandparents – and transgenerational trauma, if you like, is the trauma that is passed down through culture and through society.

When we have unresolved trauma of any description, our ability to connect with others becomes disrupted.

So if trauma is being passed down the generations, through our family systems, and across the generations, in society and in our culture, then we are also inheriting inabilities to connect with others. And this serves to make us feel even more isolated, alone and separate in our lives. Also, with trauma we create a narrative – and this narrative can be passed down through the generations. Unfortunately, the narrative created by our trauma does not help us to heal it.

If we look back and scan generations before us, it is not difficult to spot that we have become more disconnected as a species than ever.

In the past, most of us, certainly in the West, have been taught that if something bad or difficult happens, either to us or within the family unit, that it is best to forget about it – to brush it under the carpet.

But what we know now is that even when we do ignore or "forget" our difficult experiences, by not fully processing them, or by keeping them a secret, our bodies don't forget. And these experiences remain unprocessed in our system and *can then be passed down to our children.*

And our parents and grandparents will have passed down some of their trauma to us too.

Emily arrived to see me aged 45, and she was constantly stressed, crying a lot, and unable to function in her adult self around her children or in her life. She had a relatively privileged upbringing by most standards, but her parents were emotionally unavailable. As a result of this, her child psyche had stored up a tidal wave of emotion that was bleeding out into her everyday life. A few months into the work, it became apparent that the target we were working on was not actually unresolved trauma from Emily's own life. Previously in our sessions, she had processed a huge amount around what actually had happened in her childhood, and how she had experienced it at the time. But her presentation this time was slightly different; it was heavy, it was deep, and in the image that we were working on, with her as a little girl, Mum was shouting. Emily had already processed the shock and the terror around Mum shouting in previous sessions, but there was something else going on, deep in her system, that didn't want to shift. I changed the focus of the session on to her mother, still in the memory, and we worked on Mum directly. We found Mum as a child, separated from her parents, in a different country, feeling lost and abandoned. We processed this and the session was beautiful and complete, and Emily felt as though she had shed a whole load of emotion that, despite feeling as though it was hers, had actually belonged to her mother. She had internalised her mother's unprocessed past experiences as her own. No wonder if felt so enormous. What was really interesting too was that, whilst Emily was imagining her younger mother, in India, alone, with no parents, she could also smell the poverty and the spices of India very vividly. She was shocked at this, and asked me at the end of the session: "How was it that I could smell the poverty and spices in India, when I've never even been there myself?"

Epigenetics and generational trauma

One of the answers to Emily's question lies in the extraordinary work of epigenetics.

The concept that the epigenetics community has discovered is very simple – even if the biological processes taking place in the genes are incredibly complex.

In a short summary, the basic need-to-know information is this:

- Unresolved trauma changes how our DNA is expressed.
- These changes to the DNA expression can be passed down to our children.

We can pass unresolved trauma down the generations via our DNA. And we do.

This epigenetic work began by studying the adult children of Holocaust survivors; in other words, the children who did not even experience the Holocaust – but whose parents did.

It was found that many of these adult children of Holocaust survivors suffered either with PTSD, or anxiety, or depression, along with feelings of excessive guilt, morbid grief, feeling a burden of compensating for past losses, problems separating from and / or confronting their parents, and of course relationship difficulties in their lives as a result. Hopefully now, from reading this book, we can recognise that all of these states are signs and symptoms of unresolved trauma. Many of these people also had the feeling that some of what they were carrying did not belong to them, and that it was not affiliated with anything that had happened to them personally in their lifetimes. But they were at a loss as to how they could feel better.

Some of their feelings and beliefs will have been passed down through behaviour patterns and inherited belief systems of their Holocaust survivor parents, as we have talked about earlier in the chapter. But what the epigenetic community has found is that the DNA expression modifications in the parents, that were sparked by the traumatic events of the Holocaust, were also passed down to the children.

The trauma of the Holocaust was passed down to the children of the Holocaust survivors, via the DNA.

This passing down of DNA expression "alterations" can occur both in the sperm and in the egg – in other words, from both of the parents. As DNA replicates in the body – as it does all the time – the expression alterations from any unresolved trauma remains the same. So, the egg and the sperm of a parent with unresolved trauma can carry this unresolved experience, via the DNA, to their child.

It gets even more crazy. Let's just think about an adult female experiencing a traumatic event when she is pregnant, or feeling the effects of her generational trauma whilst pregnant. When this occurs, the alterations to this adult female's DNA expression will not only occur inside her, but they will also occur in the DNA expression of the baby she is carrying and – wait for it – also into the *ova* of the foetus that she is carrying; because they will all have some of the same DNA.

In other words, if we are female and we endure something traumatic whilst we are pregnant that we do not fully process, or we already have unresolved trauma in our system, then we can also pass that unresolved traumatic experience *down to our grandchildren* via our DNA.

Let's just pause for a moment and think back to our grandparents and the big traumas that they might have endured. Many of us will have had grandparents in the First or Second World Wars and, depending on what country we live in, other wars besides. I wonder how much of their wartime, unresolved trauma we might be carrying.

But of course, inherited trauma is not limited to war. ANY unresolved trauma – both Big T trauma and developmental trauma – can be passed down to the future generations via the DNA. We can see how this looks a bit more clearly from Lucille's case study:

Lucille had done a lot of trauma healing work over the past few years, but she still felt a heaviness inside her that she couldn't properly shift; a sadness. She couldn't understand why she felt so incredibly sad. She was perfectly able to function as her adult self, and she reckoned that most of her childhood trauma had properly been looked at, processed and healed. On top of this, she really liked her life – she loved her work, and she loved her husband and her children. But this deep feeling of sadness in her chest increased over time, and we had a look at it when she was ready. Her readiness to look at it presented as a really entrenched and painful belief: "I don't want to live anymore, I can't bear this feeling anymore, I'd rather be dead". She didn't want to kill herself for the sake of her children, but the thought of her children was the only thing stopping her at this point.

We found her younger self, and as she connected with her numbness as a very young child, it was suggested in the session "Where is Mum?" and again the session was turned towards Mum as a child. Turns out Mum was five years old, feeling alone, feeling separate from and unable to connect with her siblings; feeling jealous of them, yearning for a sense of connection. Lucille's mum, as a youngster in the memory, was experiencing the devastating loss around her father dying in the war when she was a baby, her siblings having a different father to her, and the unavailability of her own mother. When we looked at where Lucille's mum's mother (Lucille's grandmother) might have been, we found her crying in her bedroom, aged in her early to mid twenties, grieving the loss of her first husband and also the loss of her first baby, who had died at only a few weeks old, before Lucille's mother had even been born. Lucille cried her eyes out in this session – possibly cried her guts out. It was incredibly somatic, often with what felt like an exorcism of grief leaving her body, as she processed these enormous emotions.

Lucille had been carrying the unresolved grief of her mother, and also of her grandmother, for the whole 45 years of her life.

She had been carrying over 100 years of unresolved grief inside her – perhaps more. No wonder she felt as though she wanted to die. That is way too much for a human's psyche to have to tolerate.

The following session, Lucille connected with the grief of her father that had also been buried deep inside him, and she was able to release that too. She felt pretty reborn after those two sessions.

So we can see, from both Emily and Lucille, that generational trauma is not limited to Holocaust survivors. The Holocaust survivors' adult children study has been an incredibly important area of research where trauma and epigenetics could be properly examined. But the theory that we pass unresolved experiences down the generations, via the gene expression alterations in the DNA, remains the same for any type of unresolved trauma that we might be carrying, be it a big trauma, or developmental trauma.

And this is no longer a hypothesis – it has now been proven.

Until unresolved trauma is addressed and processed – *any* unresolved trauma – it can continue to be passed down, through the generations, either maternally to each baby that is born and to each ovary in every foetus, or paternally via the sperm.

The really good news though

We see from these case studies (and many more clients than just these two) that *we can heal* these heavy burdens that have been passed to us from the generations before us. And there are amazing healing modalities out there whose practitioners also experience the same with their clients.

There's good news from this epigenetic standpoint too: when this unresolved trauma is processed, *the gene expression alterations of the DNA change again to reflect this.* Isn't that just amazing?

This is some of the science behind the two case studies, Emily and Lucille. Both of these women show us that we can still heal by processing our generational trauma.

And there are trauma therapists all over the world helping people to heal their generational trauma. It's just not talked about enough in the mainstream, yet, which is why many people don't know about it.

When we do the trauma work, we are working with the imprint left on the cells. Because of neuroplasticity, and the make-up of DNA, we can actually neutralise the emotional impact of that imprint through trauma work. We are not changing what happened – of course we cannot go back in time to do that – but we can change the imprint on our cells that has been passed down. We can change and heal our altered gene expression.

And by doing this, not only do we heal ourselves, but we prevent our unresolved trauma from being passed down to the generation after us.

Healing our ancestors

There is, and has been for many years, a deeply held belief that when we heal ourselves, we also heal our ancestors.

I am not going enter into this discussion in any depth, because for some it can feel a bit too "woo-woo" and "out there". And we do not even need to go there. Many clients, who have healed their trauma around their parents, report a much more improved relationship with said parents.

Abby, aged 45, had been doing the inner work for some time. She reported, in one session, that not only did she not feel triggered around her mother anymore, but also that her mother was behaving in a more kind and compassionate way towards her. Abby could not believe it. Her mother had been cold and shut down throughout all of Abby's childhood, and well into Abby's adulthood too. And much of the work we had done together was centred around Abby's ruptured attachment relationship with Mum. But recently, her mother had appeared warmer. For the first time in Abby's life, her mother would make supportive comments or suggestions to Abby. Abby felt, for the first time in her life, as though she actually had a mother.

So what is going on here? We knew that Abby's mother had never set foot in a therapist's office, so we knew that she had not had any trauma therapy. Yet her outlook towards Abby was appearing to change. Why is this?

If we think back to Chapter 4, we will remember that much of our childhood trauma is a result of our parents acting out their own unresolved trauma. This provides a dynamic where we feel disconnected.

Just because our parents traumatised us without realising consciously that they were doing so, however, does not mean that deep down they will have felt OK about it. On the contrary, even on an unconscious level, if we have caused someone else some harm, we will have a sense that we have done so. And in the case of a parent, we will feel a degree of guilt or shame around it.

Let's imagine ourselves in the role of a parent for a moment. If our child grows up and is clearly unhappy, we will certainly notice that. And we feel powerless to change it. We might even know, on an unconscious level, that some of it will have been our doing. It will gnaw at us inside even if we cannot put our finger on why. And it will most probably trigger us into our feelings of "I am not good enough", as well.

If our child, now an adult, begins to heal their hurt, then we will witness them feeling happier; we will notice this. And once we do, we will no longer feel so triggered by them. We will no longer feel responsible for their happiness, or on some level ashamed, because we sort of knew that we were party to their discomfort. At last, we will be able to relax, because our child is well.

This was the case for Abby's mother. Seeing Abby well, and happy, was a huge relief for her. She had no idea why, not consciously, but something had relaxed in her system seeing her daughter doing so well, seeing her daughter thriving.

This phenomenon is not solely occurring in the life of Abby either. It occurs for many people who have had some trauma recovery. They are now experiencing stronger relationships with other family members, despite those other family members not having had any therapy themselves.

This is, to my mind, a beautiful demonstration of how our own healing can help to heal the generations that came before us, without a whisper of the "woo-woo" in sight.

Stigma also keeps trauma hidden

In addition to the generational aspects of passing trauma on unnoticed, there is more that keeps our trauma hidden.

A huge part of our societal trauma is that there is still a stigma around most psychological and emotional suffering.

This drastically needs to change.

This stigma prevents people who are suffering from asking for help.

This stigma also keeps the families of the people suffering stuck in their dysfunction. In Chapter 7, we look at the functionality of the family system. Very often it is family members who ridicule the notion of outside help and instead push everything onto the member of the family who is obviously suffering.

Stigma around psychological struggles exists everywhere. In the individual, in the family system, in society at large, and in many cultures.

And it remains hidden

And this unresolved trauma remains hidden.

Many people still ridicule the notion of trauma. Many people love their defences too much to want to change.

For some, any type of self-reflection is still considered "self-indulgent", or "selfish", "self-obsessed", or even "self-seeking".

Many more people violently oppose therapy, or still hold a stigma around asking for professional help.

Mastin Kipp, the author of *Claim Your Power*, eloquently said "therapy should be as normal as going to the gym". And I agree with him. I would take it a step further and say that *"trauma* therapy should be as normal as going to the gym".

Currently, however, it is sadly the case that it is the signs and symptoms of trauma that are as "as normal as going to the gym", not the actual trauma therapy.

But more and more, as science evolves, as communication accelerates, and as we evolve as humans, people are realising the effects of unresolved trauma (childhood or otherwise) as self-evident. We need to keep this going, not least for ourselves, but also for the future generations.

We simply are not aware that many of our behaviours are in fact trauma responses, or our (or our parents') adaptations to trauma – they are just our "normal".

Perhaps we have inherited maladaptive behaviours or beliefs from our family system, and they are viewed as our "normal".

Perhaps we are carrying the previous generations' unresolved trauma and it very much feels a "normal" part of ourselves.

By now, we can see a bit more clearly how this epidemic has occurred, and how it has managed to remain so well hidden.

Shame

And next, as promised a chapter ago, we will look at another enormous reason why our trauma remains hidden.

And this reason is shame.

CHAPTER 6

Shame

In the last two chapters, we talked about how trauma has happened and how it has stayed hidden, and we were able to see how our parents' unresolved trauma resulted in us not getting everything that we needed as children. We learned how the same happened with our parents, and their parents before them, and how unresolved events and experiences can be passed down through the generations. We also looked at how unresolved trauma is normalised within the family and within societies. How we have found ourselves in an epidemic of unresolved trauma is probably making a bit more sense now.

But there is another enormous factor that keeps us from realising our hurt, and, in a heartbreaking number of cases, also prevents us from reaching out and asking for help.

And that other enormous factor is shame. Therefore, when we are learning about trauma and we want to heal, we need to also learn about shame.

Shame can keep us hiding in our pain, terrified in our trauma, and shame can prevent us from healing. Let's take a look.

What is shame?

We have all felt shame before, that icky, shuddery, all-encompassing, curling up hideousness, that feeling of wanting the ground to swallow us up. That feeling of wanting to be hidden, wanting to hide. Needing to be hidden, needing to hide. Please don't see me. I am bad. There is something fundamentally wrong with me. I need to disappear.

Shame is a horrendous feeling. It is hot, deep, visceral, extraordinarily uncomfortable – and an emotion we will do almost anything to avoid experiencing.

When we feel shame, we also carry negative beliefs about ourselves – they go hand in hand. Let's think back to Chapter 2 and the negative cognitions that we can have towards ourselves. Any of those negative beliefs that suggest we are defective, in any way, are related to our feelings of shame. For example:

I am not lovable
I am not worth it
I am not worth as much as so-and-so
I am shameful
I am bad
I am dirty
I'm worthless
I am not enough
I'm not good enough
I am wrong
Others must be right and I'm wrong
I will never be enough
I am damaged

I am permanently damaged
I'm defective
I'm ugly
There is something wrong with me
I am not good enough

All of the above negative cognitions suggest that there is something wrong with us in our core. Not that we have done something wrong, but that we *are* wrong. Not "I have done a bad thing", but "*I am* bad". Not "that piece of work I just delivered wasn't quite good enough", but "*I am not* good enough".

If we allow ourselves to think about it for a moment, when we think about those beliefs towards ourselves, we will realise that we are carrying a feeling of shame along with them.

Shame is not the same as guilt. Guilt is "Oh, I feel so guilty, I forgot to RSVP in time"; in other words, I have done something that does not fit with my value system, and I feel guilty about it. I have done something wrong. But I can correct it by taking action in order to not feel this feeling anymore.

Shame, on the other hand, is a feeling that there is something wrong with us. We are bad. I am bad. There is something wrong with me.

Guilt: "I have done something wrong" (and I can correct it)

Shame: "I am wrong" (and there's nothing I can do about it)

The shame we are referring to here is "toxic shame".

This toxic shame is corrosive. It makes us feel *wrong*. We feel there is something wrong with us. And it doesn't even occur to us that we can change that feeling, because it runs so deep. We feel fundamentally flawed in our core, fundamentally wrong in our entire being. Sometimes, we even feel as though we were born "wrong".

Another negative belief that we often carry with the feeling of shame is "It is my fault". It is my fault that I am wrong, unlovable, or unworthy, or bad.

But before we feel despondent about this, there is good news. We do not need to feel this toxic shame. We can clear it. We can release it. We don't need to carry it, and we certainly don't need to have it dictating our lives. Ever.

Because it is not our shame. It does not belong to us. We can free ourselves from the burden of this toxic shame. I will come on to this later.

The evolutionary purpose of shame

First of all, let's look at why we have shame – in other words, what is the purpose of shame?

To get to grips with understanding this corrosive emotion, we first need to realise that there is healthy shame as well as this toxic shame. Shame is a very important "relational" feeling – in other words, it plays a big part in how we relate with others.

Let's look at healthy shame first.

Healthy shame: Little Jonny kicked his brother in the ankle, and his brother cried and cried. Little Jonny can see how much his brother is hurting. Little Jonny feels ashamed that he hurt his brother, as he learns to empathise with his brother's pain and his tears. This is healthy shame. Little Jonny then learns that it's not nice to kick, because kicking hurts people, and this makes him feel bad. So Little Jonny won't kick again, because he doesn't want to feel that "bad" again – he doesn't want to feel ashamed again. Little Jonny is learning healthy shame. This is good! This is healthy. Sometimes, as adults, when our behaviours are less than optimum, we might feel ashamed. And we probably won't do that thing again. "I felt really ashamed of myself for falling down drunk at the wedding." Yeah, that's going to feel horrible. But we can make amends, we can forgive ourselves, and we can take the lesson; "I won't be doing that again, it hurt me and it hurt others". These are all examples of healthy shame. They are things that we have done that we feel ashamed about. The healthy part of this is that we have learned not to do that thing again, because we don't want to feel that horrible feeling again.

Unhealthy shame: as already mentioned, unhealthy shame is that icky, all-encompassing, hot, inward-coiling feeling that there is something wrong with me. I am bad. I am unlovable. I am not good enough. In other words, the healthy shame has turned in on us and has become unhealthy. This is also known as "toxic shame".

So how does shame become toxic? How do we end up with this horrid, unhealthy shame that I'm telling you isn't ours in the first place?

Emergence of healthy relational shame for the young child

It is thought that children start to recognise the feeling of shame at early toddler age. As most of us probably know, a toddler's emotions encompass a wide spectrum, and a young toddler wants to please their mum, or primary caregiver. Allan Schore (2017) uses the example of poo to describe relational shame. Imagine Little Jonny is 15 months old and accustomed to playing with Mum and having Mum mirror back his joy to him. He rushes into the room one day, ecstatic, beaming, highly aroused with positive emotion, excited to show Mum what he has found. But instead of it being a beautiful leaf, or a toy, this time he has found some poo and is presenting the poo to his mum. Mum's initial shock reaction to the poo will be that of horror. In that moment of witnessing Mum's horror, Little Jonny's emotions will crash right to the bottom end of the scale, as he mirrors and picks up on Mum's expression and feelings.

It is believed that this enormous leap from the highest positive emotions right down to the lowest of the negative emotions, during those critical years of right-brain presence, especially around Mum to begin with, elicits the feeling of relational shame. More on the right brain and Mum in Chapter 9. Hopefully, Mum will recover from the shock quickly and will be able to help Little Jonny to regulate his emotions "up" again. Once Little Jonny is regulated, Mum will calmly and firmly tell him that poo isn't to be brought into the house. This will enable Little Jonny to feel safe, even though Mum is displeased. Little Jonny is beginning to develop healthy, or relational shame.

Shame is a powerful emotion. In its healthy, relational sense, it is paramount to evolution, it stops us from killing other people. When we are young, we know that Mum will be displeased by our "wrong" actions, and as we develop our own sense of self, the relational shame grows, and we realise for ourselves that we don't want to hurt other people. We can probably all imagine that if we killed a fellow human, we would feel dreadful on many levels – we would feel deep shame. Therefore, we don't kill people. This is when our shame is healthy, relational and helpful, and very, very necessary – when it stops us from killing other people. Essentially, shame is moderating our behaviour around other beings. And that is the evolutionary purpose of shame – in its essence it will help us relate to people in a considerate manner, and it will stop us from killing other people, in order that evolution can continue.

Another evolutionary purpose of healthy or relational shame is to keep us feeling part of the pack, part of the tribe, or part of our family or society. As humans, we have a deep desire to feel "part of", to feel connected to others. If we think back to Chapter 4 and the Jim Knipe diagrams, we might remember that we change ourselves in order to fit in with the family system and our parents' expectations. In order to do this, we have to make our parents "right". If we realised that Mum and Dad were actually wrong when they told us, or implied, that we were not good enough, then we would lose our sense of safety in the family system, and that would be too terrifying a prospect. So we make our parents right – regardless of their behaviours – and we choose to make ourselves the "wrong" ones. We choose to feel the shame that accompanies that, rather than lose our sense of belonging to our family in order to ensure we are fed, watered, clothed and looked after emotionally.

All the main feeling groups have an evolutionary purpose. Love propels us to procreate – thus allowing evolution. Fear gets us out of danger and helps to prevent us being killed – thus allowing evolution. Shame prevents us from killing our fellow humans and keeps us feeling part of the pack and subsequently our physical and emotional survival – again, allowing evolution.

So, healthy relational shame has an important purpose for evolution.

Owning our healthy shame

We have to own our healthy shame in order for it to do its evolutionary job. For example, if we decide not to murder another person, then we are owning our healthy shame – and that ownership of our healthy shame prevents us from killing people, thus allowing the species to evolve. To own our healthy shame is, if you like, to act in accordance with it. So how do people murder other people? By not owning their sense of healthy shame, that's how.

We can probably all see how murdering someone is a shameful thing to do. It is a shameful act to take the life of another.

Another shameful act that we probably all recognise is that of abusing someone sexually.

Anyone who sexually abuses another person is not going to be owning their healthy shame, which is why they are able to do it. Very likely they have no concept of healthy shame; perhaps they were not taught it sufficiently when they were younger.

If perpetrators owned their healthy shame around sexual abuse, they would not perform the abuse and they would not be perpetrators of abuse. And I'm going to use this example to explain the transfer of shame which is so important to understand when we're talking about shame in the context of trauma.

Transfer of shame

When someone – let's call them the perpetrator – commits an act of sexual abuse, it is a shameful act. However, despite it being a shameful act, the perpetrator of the abuse – the abuser – is not owning their healthy shame; if they were, they would not be committing the abuse. Therefore, the perpetrator is partaking in a shameful act, because they are not owning their own healthy shame.

Emotions are energy, as we have already discussed (e-motion = energy in motion). Because sexual abuse is a shameful act in and of itself, there is still shame *in the ether* whilst the act is being committed. Given there is shame in the ether, because sexual abuse is a shameful act, and because the shame is not owned by the perpetrator, then the shame is transferred to the victim. The victim, the receiver of the sexual abuse, takes on that shame as if it were their own. And this is the toxic shame to which I referred earlier.

Every single person I have met who has been sexually abused feels shame around the abuse, and as a result of the abuse, no matter if they were four years old, 14 years old, or 44 years old when it happened. This is because sexual abuse is a shameful act, and the shame is not owned by the abuser. *Therefore, the shame gets taken on by – or transferred to – the victim.* And the victim feels the shame. The abused feels the shame of the shameful act, even though it is the abuser doing the shameful act, not the abused. It feels desperately unfair, but that is what happens.

If you are reading this and you have been sexually abused and you feel shame, however much you feel that it is your shame, I promise you it is not your shame. The shame you feel around being sexually abused belongs to your abuser, not you.

Chapter 8 covers sexual abuse in much more detail.

Other shameful acts

We've talked about two shameful acts so far – killing someone and sexually abusing someone.

When someone is sexually abused, they will most likely feel shame, whatever the age they were abused.

But there are other shameful acts too – ones that we perhaps don't realise are shameful. And if these are committed when we are young, during our childhoods, then we will end up taking on that shame.

To shame a child is to traumatise a child.

Do you remember the example of Little Jonny running out into the road in Chapter 3? Mummy, in shock and panicking, hauls him back on to the pavement and shouts at him for running into the road.

How did Little Jonny feel when Mummy shouted? He felt "bad". He felt "unlovable". He felt wrong. He felt like there was something wrong with him. He felt shame.

Shouting at a child is a shameful act. When we shout at a child, the child feels "bad". That's a child's way of describing shame: "I feel bad". And if it happens often enough, that child will have such a large shame bank that they will internalise the feeling of "I am bad", or "there is something wrong with me" and it will feel very, very true for them. But the child has not done anything shameful at all! All they have done is acted like a normal child! And they have been shouted at for it! But during those first few years of life, when our neural pathways are forming and our left brain is not yet properly online, if we internalise those shame-based negative beliefs, then they stick; that's how brain development in our early years works.

If we shout at a child and immediately apologise and say "I am so sorry, I flipped my lid. You didn't deserve that, this is my stuff not yours. I am so sorry." And then when they have calmed down, we can add "We can't have that behaviour, but you didn't deserve me shouting at you", then we are owning our shame – we are taking it back again – and the child will consequently not take the shame on as theirs. We can correct our behaviour, and by doing so we prevent those neural pathways from wiring in a shame-based manner. If we shout at children all the time and then apologise like that all the time, then the child will probably learn that we are a bit odd. But they won't end up feeling "I am bad". They might feel "Mum's / Dad's a bit crazy, and I feel really scared when she / he yells", but they won't take on the shame nearly so much, because we have immediately owned it, we've immediately taken it back before it can get lodged in our child. Our child won't end up fundamentally believing that there is something wrong with them. Provided there are no other shameful acts committed, of course.

Let's look at some other acts that make children feel shame.

Other shameful acts towards children

Below are some more examples of shameful adult behaviour towards a child that will result in a child feeling as though there is something wrong with them, feeling shame:

- Talking negatively about a child in front of them
- Putting a child down
- Insulting a child
- Swearing at a child
- Hitting a child
- Threatening any type of physical punishment
- Telling a child that it's their fault you are in a bad mood
- Telling a child that they are not good enough at something
- Making a child wear clothes that they simply hate
- Making a child wear clothes inappropriate for their age
- Telling a child that they need to lose weight
- Telling a child that they need to gain weight
- Comparing a child to another child
- Putting excessive pressure on a child to do well in school
- Parental expectations put on a child that do not

resonate with the child
- Saying "don't be so stupid"
- Any punishment that doesn't fit the crime
- Saying: "stop crying", "don't be a crybaby", "grow up" or "big boys don't cry" or "big girls don't cry"
- Any invalidation of their emotions
- Any invalidation of their inner state ("you can't be hungry, we only had lunch an hour ago", for example)
- Saying: "you're so naughty", "I don't know what to do with you", "I can't cope with you"
- Not allowing a child to do things for themselves when they want to try
- Judging a child's choices: "I can't believe you just did that", or "what were you thinking?"
- Laughing at a child
- Regularly using a harsh tone with a child
- Saying: "you're hopeless"
- Saying: "look at how much I've given up for you", "look at how much I do for you"
- And if any of the above happens to a child in public, in front of other people, the child will receive a double whammy of shame.

It's quite a list, isn't it – and of course this is not exhaustive. Perhaps you can think of even more examples now you get the drift. And look at how "normal" some of these behaviours towards children are. We can call it "shaming".

And if we were shamed this way as children – which many, many of us were, we will feel so "normal" carrying around that shame that we will most likely do the same to our children because it will feel so normal to us.

But if you ever witness a child who has never felt "shamed", then you will notice that this child will be appalled to see or hear any of those above things happening to a child. How do I know this? Because after people have healed their toxic shame, they will spot it in others, and it will make them cringe in their core to hear a child being shamed.

If we are shamed and it is not corrected by the people who shamed us, we will carry this toxic shame in our system, unresolved and unprocessed, making us feel as though there is fundamentally something wrong with us. And we will carry this into our adult lives.

When we carry toxic shame, instead of keeping us alive it makes us feel as though we should die, as though there is something terribly wrong with us, as though we are mentally ill. When we carry toxic shame, instead of it helping us to relate to other people, it drives a wedge between us and them, causing us to feel even more separate and disconnected.

Other ways we feel shame

Let's think back to those 4 Ss we have talked about – Seen, Soothed, Safe, Secure. Because we will also feel some shame if there was an *absence* of the amount of kindness, compassion, warmth, unconditional love and safety that we needed for optimum emotional health. If we had a parent who didn't see us for exactly who we were, and how we were, at any given moment, enough of the time when we were younger, we will have developed a feeling of unworthiness around who we are in our essence. If we were not soothed when we were upset, enough of the time, as a child, here again we will develop a sense that we are not worthy, we are not worth it, we do not count – our feelings do not count. Feelings of unworthiness come from our feeling of toxic shame.

Any shameful acts done to a child, or an absence of enough of the 4 Ss, or any combination of the two, makes a child feel worthless, unloved, bad, wrong, undeserving and not good enough. And if this happens regularly during childhood, then we end up with a whole host of these shame-based, negative self-beliefs that we will carry into our adult lives.

We very often also think it is our fault. We think there is something wrong with us that we are treated this way. If we had enough of this happen to us before the age of seven or eight, or in our early teens – in other words when our brains are really elastic – then we will carry those negative self-beliefs right into adulthood. Right up until we do trauma-informed therapy, or the trauma work itself.

And it becomes our normal to feel like this. That feeling of shame becomes our normal. Those beliefs we have about ourselves become our normal. Even though we are carrying our parents' or teachers' or abusers' shame, *we don't realise it is theirs because it Feels. Like. It. Is. Ours.*

But it's not our shame. Those significant adults don't realise that they are shaming the children. We don't realise that we were shamed. We don't realise that we are shaming our children. We don't realise that we are carrying other people's shame, and we don't realise that we are transferring our own shame to our children.

Children have been shamed for years and years and years. And years and years and years. And a parent who was shamed will most probably shame their child, because they simply won't know any different.

If we are going to understand trauma, heal from it, and prevent it from being passed down the generations, then we have to understand exactly what constitutes a shameful act.

We also need to understand that any toxic shame we feel in our core actually belongs to the person who shamed us, not to us. Once we fully understand this, then we are better placed to release that shame and hand it back to the people who gave it to us.

Any shame that our child feels in their core is a result of us shaming them. Here we need to take back that shame from our child, by explaining that we were wrong to say what we did, or react how we did, and that we are sorry, and that they absolutely did not deserve that. We need to really learn what constitutes a shameful act, and we need to stop doing those things.

Shaming as discipline

Parents often resort to shaming when they feel they can't control their children – very often when they feel immensely triggered by their children. In other words, a parent's buttons are pressed by their children, and there is a strong sense in the parent of "I can't cope". It is in these moments that parents very often resort to shaming. And of course, because they were shamed by their parents – and their parents by their parents before them – they are all already carrying toxic shame themselves.

It is now illegal, but in the past children were caned for disciplinary purposes at school, or at home. What a shameful act it is, caning a child. It's not a surprise that it is now illegal.

Before now, we have not fully understood at all the negative impact that shaming is having on our children. But we do now. And we must do something about it.

Let's just take a moment and think about it. When we were shamed when we were little, how did it feel? Who did it to us? Was it a regular occurrence or just occasional? Did we harden ourselves to it because it happened so often? After a while of being shamed, we will have hardened ourselves to cope with it – we will have built a wall of protection around ourselves to protect us from the horrid, horrid feelings. Let's just see if we can allow ourselves to remember what it felt like to be shamed before we had built up this wall of protection.

We may not be able to, because we have built up so many layers of protection around it. It can feel incredibly difficult to allow ourselves to feel that shame because, on one level, it feels like we might die if we do. Remember, healthy shame prevents us from killing others. So if it is turned in on us, we could feel like we will die.

Symptoms of shame

We know that, with shame, we carry negative self-beliefs that revolve around the notion that we are defective, but there are also ways in which we might act when we carry shame. Let's have a look now at some of the ways in which shame might show up in our behaviours. You might notice that they all revolve around a fear of people seeing who we truly are – because we feel shame.

Lying. We feel too ashamed of who we are, so we tell lies. We feel not good enough, so we make up stories – or exaggerate truths – in order that people will think more of us, or to make our story more believable. Sometimes we feel ashamed of the lies we have told, and we pretend to ourselves that we have not lied in order to avoid having to feel that horrible feeling of shame. Very often, when we have toxic shame, we lie to ourselves too.

Masks. We wear masks in order that people don't see the real us, so that they don't see the awfulness that we think we are if anyone were to see the real us. Masks are also a way of lying, and a way that the lies have become our "normal". We also find other people – friends – who have similar masks to us, so that we don't need to examine our masks. If others wear the same mask, we reason, "then it must be OK".

Secretive behaviour. We keep secrets about who we feel we are, and how we are, because we feel so ashamed of who we are. We smoke in secret. We drink in secret. We do all sorts of things in secret.

Not asking for help. We suffer in silence, because we feel too ashamed of not being able to cope, or we feel ashamed of anyone seeing that we can't cope.

Staying in relationships that are not working any longer. We stay in relationships that are not working for us, because we constantly think we must be doing something wrong and that the other person must be right. If they say we are hopeless, then we must be. We have a niggle that there is something amiss with them too, but we ignore it because our own shame tells us that it must be all our fault.

Not trusting ourselves. When we are shamed and we feel "wrong" when we are young, we learn that our own instinct is not right – and that our own feelings are not "right". We then stop listening to the inner voice of our truth. If our truth has been deemed "wrong" by a significant adult in childhood, then we will learn that it is not to be trusted. So by adulthood, we will have learned that our authentic thoughts and feelings don't count. So we stop listening to them, until we just don't hear them anymore.

Anger. Very often people react with anger to cover up shame. It is easier to blame others than to think we might have done something wrong. A narcissistic person, for example, will rage and turn everything against the other, because of their extraordinarily well-hidden feelings of deep shame.

Addiction. Many people will resort to external substances to cover up their deep feelings of unworthiness (shame). In extreme examples of addiction, they will then become ashamed of their using and use even more in an attempt to hide that shame.

Depression. The negative beliefs that come with the feeling of shame can easily lead someone into depression, and if they are all-encompassing will almost certainly do so. If we are suffering from depression, we will have shame-based beliefs at our core.

Shame, specifically being shamed, has contributed to our trauma. And very often this toxic shame prevents us from believing we can heal.

And it's not even our shame.

Healing our shame

Unresolved, toxic shame in our systems, is unresolved trauma. It is toxic in the body. It is unprocessed, because it does not belong to us. It leaves a trauma imprint on us. Luckily, we can heal.

Very often, during trauma therapy, feelings of shame will be released automatically, once we have an understanding that it is not our shame that we are feeling – in other words, once we have an understanding around what toxic shame really is. Sometimes in a session, once we have identified and experienced the feeling of shame in our system, we might physically hand back the shame to our abuser.

And then we don't feel the shame any longer.

We need to give this shame back to the person it belongs to. We need to release it from inside us.

Next time you feel toxic shame, ask yourself "Whose shame is this?"

Next time you feel not good enough, or unlovable, ask yourself "Whose shame is this?" Who made me feel like this when I was younger? Where does this negative belief come from?

Because it is not your shame. You can give it back. You don't need to carry it anymore.

If this feels too difficult to do on your own, please find a trauma therapist and ask for their help.

You don't need to carry it anymore.

Societal shame

Brené Brown, in her now renowned TED talk on shame, speaks about her research findings on the subject. When she interviewed women about the qualities to which they aspired, the responses she received were: nice, thin, modest, using all available resources for appearance. All of those things that Brené's respondents aspired to, have shame as the underbelly: I am not enough as I am; there is something wrong with me; I cannot shine my light; I must not speak up. And for men it was just as alarming. When she interviewed men, the top things that they aspired to were show emotional control, work is first, pursue status, and violence.

All of these aspirations, for both men and women, are shame-based aspirations, because they all suggest that, in our essence, we are not enough.

But we are enough. We just are. We are all beautiful beings of light! But if we have layers of toxic shame inside us, from hideous things that happened to us, or from the loving things that didn't happen for us, then we can't fully access our inner light. If this is compounded by how we are viewed in society, or by how we think society views us, it is incredibly difficult to escape the feeling of toxic shame without doing some serious inner healing.

Teenage societal shaming

Even if we have escaped our early childhoods relatively unscathed by shame, when we hit the age where we are much more aware of our surroundings we are usually in our early teens. In our early teens, the brain goes through another stage of neuroplasticity. In other words, we once again become very susceptible to external views.

Given our age, we are now even more awake to the societal shaming that can occur.

This shaming can exist in schools with the incredible pressure to succeed – to fit into a system regardless of our character and personality. The exam pressure, university and further education pressure, social media pressure. All of these external pressures feed that core notion that we are not enough as we are. They contribute to our toxic shame.

Given this new stage of neuroplasticity at the start of our teenage years, we are very susceptible to societal shaming. And if our parents have succumbed to this societal shaming already, then we will be even more open to being wounded by it. It will feel very "normal" to accept feelings of being shamed.

To heal from our shame, we need to do the inner work ourselves.

But even more than that, we need to heal our societal shame too.

Our first step in healing is in recognising that when we carry toxic shame it is hijacking our sense of self. It makes us feel as though there is something wrong with us; that is its very nature. But there isn't anything wrong with us. That is the toxic shame talking, not the truth. Our first step is beginning to understand that it is not our shame.

CHAPTER 7

Dysfunctional families

In Chapters 4 and 5 we looked at why this epidemic and normalisation of trauma has happened, and how it has managed to stay hidden. If we take a minute to examine the family system, we can further understand this phenomenon.

How many of us have heard a parent or family member say, at some point, "he's so tricky", "she's so sensitive", "so-and-so gives us nothing but trouble" or "yeah, they're the one with the problems / issues". Or perhaps we have heard people – or us – being described as "oversensitive" or "difficult" or "complicated", or "too much".

Many, many people, whatever their age, whether child, teen or adult – have been told something along these lines at some point and, in the case of child clients, have often been referred to therapy by a parent as the "problem child". Nearly everyone I see has come to be known as the "odd" one in the family, the problem person, the sick one – sometimes even the "crazy" one. And yes, these people do have demons and have often developed some sort of difficulty in their lives that is regarded as a mental illness (anxiety, depression, eating disorders, addictions, self-harm, and many other psychological difficulties). What always strikes me, however – whatever their age – is how beautiful and sensitive these people are, despite their presenting difficulties, and also how their families are so often reluctant to be involved in their recovery.

So why did this happen to them rather than another family member? Why is it that this particular family member has arrived for treatment and not another? And why is it that the family is treating all of this with such disdain?

Some of the answers to these questions can be found when we look at the emotional health within a family system.

All systems – or groups – have a level of dysfunction, simply because we are rarely going to find a group of people who are all fully functioning, emotionally whole adults with little to no unresolved emotional trauma (think back to Chapter 4 and the diagrams). This deep level of personal inner enquiry has not, in the past, been a natural part of life for most people.

Family dysfunction

As with other groups, most families have some level of dysfunction because they are very rarely parented by two fully functioning, emotionally whole adults. This lack of wholeness, and inconsistent adult behaviour in the leadership, will have an effect on the emotional health of the whole family.

Every person that I see has come from a family with some level of dysfunction. Family dysfunction is very, very difficult to avoid.

I have come to see levels of family dysfunction as being on a spectrum. We can all agree that a mother / father / caregiver who regularly and overtly physically and / or sexually, and / or emotionally abuses their child is creating a dysfunctional family system. This overt, or obvious, abuse is extreme dysfunction so it's not difficult to spot, nor for us to understand it for what it is.

But dysfunction doesn't end with overt physical, sexual and emotional abuse.

A dysfunctional family is also created when this less understood emotional abuse and neglect occurs – the type of abuse I have been talking a lot about in this book; the more covert, or subtle abuse. On top of this, a dysfunctional family can, actually, very easily "function" in everyday life.

I have been trying to think of a way to describe – or rather "define" – what it means to be a dysfunctional family. Could it be an absence of love? Not really, because everyone has their own definition of love, and everyone loves their children.

It is more than love that is needed here. It comes back again to the notion of respect once more; a dysfunctional family is formed where there is a lack of respect for the members – *a lack of respect for the individuality of each member*. To respect each family member, for exactly who they are as an individual, is paramount for a healthy, functioning family. If parents can both unconditionally love and respect each of their children for their individuality, then the family has a high chance of not living in significant dysfunction. It really comes down to those 4 Ss again. If we receive those 4 Ss, enough of the time, then we are going to not only feel unconditional love from our parents and our family unit, but we are also going to feel respected for exactly who we are in our core. And our family unit will function in a very healthy manner.

One of my clients, Petra, demonstrates the difference between "love" and respect effectively: Petra took an overdose when she was 14 years old – she took 250 painkillers. She meant business. Whilst recovering in hospital, her parents took it upon themselves to read her diary, to find out why their daughter was so unhappy. Does reading someone's diary, without asking them first, show respect? Now some of you might be sitting there saying "Well of course, they had to find out, she was their daughter and they wanted to help her, and they loved her and they did it out of love". And there might be others of you reading this and saying "Whoa, not good, you don't read diaries like you don't open other people's post". And there might be more of you out there saying "Bit bloody late for that. How did they not notice before she took the pills, for God's sake!" (If you're saying that then you were most likely either raised in a more functional family, or you have enough self-awareness now to recognise that, of course, that is a truth, and that someone is suffering for a very long time – even if it's very well hidden – before they try to kill themselves.)

But back to respect. By reading Petra's diary, these parents did not show enough respect for their child who had just tried to kill herself. Now these parents most probably believed that they were reading the diary out of an act of love, and their intention will certainly have come from a place of love – desperate love. But did Petra feel loved when she heard that her parents had read her diary, despite their reasonings? No, she didn't. She felt violated, and it sent her spiralling back into self-destruction.

People can claim to act "in the name of love", but if that act is based on their version of what they regard as loving, rather than the recipient's, then it lacks understanding and it lacks respect. This act of reading Petra's diary demonstrates a lack of respect for physical and emotional boundaries. This is why I talk about respect when we talk of dysfunction, rather than solely of love.

Please do note here, this is less about the diary reading – *and more about how Petra felt about it.* Reading someone else's diary is a boundary violation, of course. We already know that her parents were out of tune with her, because she had tried – with serious intent – to kill herself. Had these parents taken time to properly get to know, nurture, love and respect Petra for exactly who she was as an individual during the 14 preceding years of her life, perhaps if they had partaken in their own trauma work and worked on themselves so that they could attune with their sensitive daughter in the way that she had needed it, then they would not have read her diary. Neither, most probably, would she have tried to kill herself.

Please remember also, that *this is not the parents' fault.* This is no-one's fault. Did those parents set out to violate their child after her overdose? Not at all. They honestly believed they were acting from a place of love and care. They just didn't know what that properly looked like for their child. And their notions on how to raise a child will have been "learned": they wouldn't have been shown deep respect by their own parents either. If we think back to Chapter 5, when we talked about trauma being passed down through the generations, we looked at how many of our behaviours are learned from our family system and from our parents. Petra's parents had learned from their own family system that children should be kept at an emotional distance for fear of spoiling them with too much love; so how on earth could they understand the importance of giving enough love, care and respect to their children? Are these parents aware that they have a level of dysfunction? No, they are not; they are in fact upstanding members of the community, who always pay their tax, have a large social group, and a relatively straightforward and full life. They would never see themselves as anything but completely functional – because logistically they function brilliantly.

But when we look at how a family functions in terms of emotional health, it doesn't matter how well a family might function logistically. Logistical functioning is very different to, and separate from, emotional functioning. If this family had been aware of their emotional dysfunction, on any level, then they would have been brushing it to the side, largely unconsciously, in order to keep up the social norms, or the generational norms, or any other "norm" that was adhered to in order for the family unit to feel safe.

So why is this dysfunction a problem for clients?

Let's look at a family dynamic. Mum and Dad get together and connect on their level of dysfunction, producing their own unique dysfunction. Mum and Dad have offspring. Some of these offspring will be comfortable enough conforming to the relative dysfunction of the parents. However, some of the offspring – one or sometimes more – will know on a very deep level, probably unconsciously, that something is not healthy within the family system. They will often sense this from the moment they are born.

Sometimes too, something traumatic might happen to that child around birth or before, or very early on in life, before they are old enough to process it fully, and they will already be viewing the world as unsafe. If we think back to Chapter 5 again, and our generational trauma, we can possibly see that if a child is born into a system carrying the unresolved grief or anxiety or shame of their parents and / or grandparents, then they are already arriving into the world with an awful lot of unprocessed emotion that does not even belong to them. And that is going to feel very heavy indeed.

Given children are predominantly right-brained, a child will pick up very early on that there is some dysfunction, and this will make the family system feel desperately uncomfortable for that child. Some people call these family members "truth seekers"; they are simply not able to brush things under the carpet at all.

Now, as this child grows up, and because every child sees their family as "normal" because that's all they know, they will immediately consider *themselves* to be the odd ones, not their family. They will feel as though they don't fit in, and they will feel like the odd one out. Their relatively dysfunctional family members will most probably make up the majority, in terms of numbers in the unit, and this will only add to the sensitive child's confusion, driving them even further into deep-seated, negative beliefs including "they must be right, I must be wrong", or "there must be something wrong with me".

A child who is happy to conform to the family dynamic will quietly accept that their needs might not be met, and will adjust themselves to meet their parents' needs relatively comfortably. If we think back to Chapter 4 again, and the diagrams demonstrating the importance of shutting down those needs that are not acceptable to our parents, we might recall how unconsciously we do this. We make agreements to fit with our parents' wishes – in order that we can form that necessary connection to the family system. Some of the children in the family unit will accomplish this without too much bother. A sensitive child, however, who can pick up on the lack of understanding and demonstration of individual, unconditional love and respect, will not be able to conform and meet the parents' needs with any degree of comfort. They will scream to get their needs met without even realising that they are doing so. This "screaming" might be loud or it might be silent, and could look like (in the absence of any autistic spectrum disorder) ongoing tantrums, refusal to conform to family rules, obsessions with certain toys or activities, obsessive-compulsive behaviours, dislike of social situations and making friends preferring instead to be alone, perfectionism, or extreme rebellion.

If a child is criticised for demonstrating any of these non-familial "traits", then the child will begin to feel ashamed of who they are as a person, and this will further drive them into feeling as though there is something wrong with them.

We can see that from a young age, the child is not fitting into the family mould. By their teens, they are most probably beginning to fit neatly into a category with a label of mental illness. This adds fuel to the family's thoughts of him / her as being the "odd one", and then "the ill one", at the same time further confirming for the suffering child that there is something wrong with them. But the truth is, all this child is doing is metaphorically screaming – in the only way that they know – that something within the family is just not quite right.

Sometimes this family member will be labelled as "weak" within the family system. However, this family member is the polar opposite of weak. This family member is actually the strongest member of the group. You are strong if you can spot a dysfunction. You are strong if you can see the truth from the outset.

Yet this child, this family member, will feel weak, helpless, and powerless, because they will feel like the minority within the group. And when a child feels as though they are in the minority, they feel as though they are the "wrong" one.

And the more wrong they feel, the more "wrong" they behave within the family unit. And, unconsciously, the family start to put a focus on that child as "difficult", "problematic" etc. There is an unconscious "ganging up" on this child. And unconsciously for the other family members, it allows them to continue in their dysfunction, because they can highlight the non-conformer as being the wrong one, which of course makes them see themselves as "right".

The Scapegoat, or the Identified Patient

This child is, what has, in the past, been referred to as, a "scapegoat". A scapegoat is someone who is an unconscious threat to the family's dysfunction. In order to prevent the family dysfunction from being discovered, all of the attention is placed on this child, and all of their suffering is highlighted and labelled as "bad", or "wrong", or "ill". Another term for this is "the identified patient".

The Origin of the Identified Patient

The term "identified patient" was coined by Gregory Bateson in the 1950s as part of the "Bateson Project" on family homeostasis. It was then further developed by other psychologists who agreed that the identified patient, or scapegoat, was generally the member of the family who was, in fact, more emotionally healthy underneath their pain than the other family members. Carl Jung spoke about the identified patient being under the influence of questions left unanswered by past generations – an impersonal karma – passed on from parents to children.

It is actually very convenient for the other family members that this person is now fitting the mould of "wrong", because by placing the focus on to the dysfunctional behaviours that this child is now displaying, the family dysfunction can remain out of the spotlight.

Unfortunately, this untreated and unhealthy family dynamic, plus the untreated trauma of the other family members, is likely to exacerbate the internal wounding for the child, making them feel even worse about themselves. The sensitive child has, on a very deep level, picked up a huge gap in the wholeness of other family members, and thus the functioning of the unit, and the child is screaming about it because they have no notion of how to articulate it. They are simply too young to do so. Their emotional and cognitive development has simply not yet reached that level of maturity.

The family members with their own dysfunction will unconsciously feel threatened by this child asking for more than they have the capacity to offer, and this is often why the sensitive child becomes the scapegoat or identified patient.

In puritanical terms, making any child a scapegoat is, actually, a form of emotional abuse. It may not be done intentionally, or consciously, but it *feels abusive to the child* because the child will feel further shamed for being who they are and for feeling how they feel. This unintended family shaming will make the child feel even more unwell, because they are then carrying the shame of the other family members too (remember in Chapter 6 – it's not your shame if it feels that deep, it belongs to another person or another group). This child will then develop survival patterns to hide the feelings of shame, and these, as we know, are generally pretty unhealthy. As we have talked about before, these survival patters can include addictions to drugs, excess alcohol, excess shopping, people-pleasing, playing around with food and workaholism, and the remainder of the list of trauma symptoms that we talked about in Chapter 2.

So, a whole heap of layers of dysfunctional behaviours, beliefs and shame are piled on to this child. No wonder they feel horrible.

Generational trauma – again

Oftentimes, this child, who is seen as the sensitive or problematic child, will be carrying intergenerational trauma from the grandparents - and even before that - as well as the parents. Carl Jung spotted this (see the "Origin of the Identified Patient" text box) decades ago, and now, with the research on generational trauma advancing at such speeds, we know that Jung was on to something very important. If we enter a family system that has a level of dysfunction, and we are carrying trauma from past generations, then we are even more likely to not feel seen or soothed, or safe or secure, because our parents will simply not understand the depth of the burden we are carrying.

Societal scapegoating

I mentioned before that this idea of the identified patient happens in many groups – not just families. It also occurs within society, and this contributes to the stigma that still surrounds mental health. Every concept we have talked about in the family dysfunction applies at a societal level.

I recently watched the movie *Joker*. Whilst an extreme example, it does show how societal dysfunction is placed conveniently on those with the more overt mental health issues. In this movie, Bruce Wayne's parents cover up his illegitimate child, and they send his mistress to a lunatic asylum with fake adoption papers. The mistress suffers unresolved trauma, because the dysfunction of the affair and its cover-up are entirely placed on to her. She is completely powerless and at the mercy of the wealthy man she has had the affair with. Consequently, her illegitimate son (the Joker) suffers severe, overt mental health problems. The beauty of *Joker* – trying to avoid a spoiler – is that the identified patients, the scapegoats, win in this case. Sadly, this victory is achieved by the Joker killing the dysfunctional, wealthy people and causing riots, which is obviously not the ideal solution. However, they do fight hard for the justice that they deserve, and the movie does make the point very well.

The importance of the family system in recovery

The understanding around and compassion for anybody who is suffering, whether they are an identified patient or not, is increasing.

But there is still a stigma around mental ill health. I do wonder how much of this stigma revolves around other family members not wanting to look at their own unresolved trauma, preferring instead to place all of the focus on someone within the system that they can, albeit at an unconscious level, control.

If we are to overcome this stigma, in order that the identified patients in the family system do have a chance to come forward and properly get well, then the family system has to change. Ideally, more members of family or societal systems need to come forward and look at their own unresolved trauma. They do have some. It is not solely the overt sufferer in the group. And if all of the focus is on the identified patient, it feels much more difficult for that person to recover.

In a dysfunctional family, where one of the children, one

of the dependents if you like, is overtly suffering and has been labelled the "sick" one, it is in fact the entire family as a whole that needs support. The family dysfunction needs to be examined and repaired in order for the child to fully recover. It is so important for us to understand, when talking about children who are having difficulties with life, that recovery is not just about the person who is in treatment. A child massively relies on their parents and other family members in order to live – not just from a logistical standpoint, but also from an emotional standpoint. Remember, this child needs to feel Seen, Soothed, Safe and Secure, unconditionally loved and respected for exactly who they are as an individual.

If they have become unwell then they are really going to struggle with recovery if the family does not also do some work. If the family does the work to heal the dysfunction, then the child will receive the 4Ss as a result and will suffer less long term damage.

It has been shown beyond doubt that children recover more quickly when their parents engage with therapy at the same time. When the parents are treated both individually and with the child, the family dysfunction can be repaired and the family system healed. This is of monumental help to the suffering child.

When parents do not engage in therapy, a child will struggle to get well and therapists so often, with a heavy heart, know that they just have to help as much as they can, hoping that when the child eventually leaves home that they will return to therapy, be able to break free and recover.

For an adult to recover however, it is less imperative that the family system changes. As an adult, we are able to – and most probably should – rely on ourselves for our basic needs and actually for many of our emotional needs too. No adult doing trauma work has needed their family to change in order that they heal their unresolved trauma, even when the parents or family members directly caused that trauma. But for a child, still ensconced in the family system, it is very different.

Compassion, understanding, kindness and unconditional love need to be given to each family member – and to the family system as a whole – so that they can begin to heal, both individually and as a unit.

So often, when the identified patient sees their other family members trying to get well too, there is an incredible leap forwards in their recovery. As the family system begins to feel more healthy, and begins to operate in a more functional manner, the child will begin to feel safe in that system. At last they will feel unconditionally loved and accepted, and they will feel Seen, Soothed, Safe and Secure. And this is the ultimate healing for the child.

But exactly the same is true of the opposite. When the identified patient's family members do not want to do the work on themselves and continue to pin all of the "problems" on the identified patient, it takes a long, long time for that person to recover. Very often they simply won't be able to do it until they are old enough to leave home.

Scapegoating a family member happens at such an unconscious level, a family will not think for a second that they are acting anything less than optimally. So the family members need to be educated. They need this psychological education. In order for this scapegoating to be stopped, there needs to be at least awareness, and at best healing, from all family members.

This is no mean feat. In some cases, we are asking families to unravel and relearn generations of "how to be" and "who to be". But if we are able to break these cycles, we can potentially make a serious leap forwards in both preventing and treating mental unwellness.

Through our own individual healing, however, we can begin to heal the family system.

CHAPTER 8

Childhood sexual trauma – a client's perspective

This book predominantly talks about developmental trauma, and this is because, as a collective, we already have a certain amount of understanding around Big T trauma. Sexual trauma, however, is a Big T trauma, regardless of what age it occurs, and there is still a lot of misunderstanding around what sexual abuse, or sexual trauma is and what constitutes it. It therefore felt important to include adult sexual abuse in this chapter too.

Many, many people suffer some sort of sexual trauma, or sexual abuse; both adults and children. It doesn't shock me anymore, because I'm used to seeing it. But from an objective standpoint, *it is shocking how many people suffer some sort of sexual abuse or sexual trauma in their lives.*

There are many gross misunderstandings, even in our modern society today, around what actually constitutes sexual trauma.

The American Psychological Association (APA) describes sexual assault as "unwanted sexual activity, with perpetrators using force, making threats, or taking advantage of victims not able to give consent".

The Crown Prosecution Service (CPS) agrees with the APA and is a great resource for information on sexual assault and sexual abuse in the UK.

Sexual assault might be rape – where there is penetrative sex (vaginal, anal or oral) without consent – and rape is truly horrendous. But sexual assault covers much more than rape too.

Sexual assault is any unwanted sexual contact or behaviour including touching or kissing, groping, grooming (doting on someone vulnerable in order to have them engage with you in a non-platonic way) and internet sexual abuse. Sexual assault can be physical and / or psychological.

This notion of "unwanted" might occur at any stage of the sexual event, but if it is there and it is expressed – either in the form of silence or protest – and it is consequently ignored, then this constitutes sexual assault.

Sexual assault is someone taking advantage of – or trying to take advantage of – another person in a sexual way.

There are no limits on race, gender, or religion when it comes to sexual abuse. It can happen to a girl, to a boy, to a man or to a woman. It can occur between strangers, friends, acquaintances, family members and current or ex-partners.

And the effects of sexual trauma, on the person who has suffered it, are immense.

In the past, there have been beliefs, especially in more

patriarchal systems, that it is OK for a man to make unwanted sexual advances towards a woman. This is one of the reasons this type of abuse has been able to continue for so long. But sexual trauma does not just exist for women. Women also sexually abuse men. As I have said, sexual abuse can be adult to adult, or adult to child – of any sex, in any combination.

When there is any type of sexual trauma, the psyche of the abused is scarred beyond anything someone who has not suffered from it could even imagine.

For some people who have been sexually assaulted, or sexually abused, they take this secret with them to the grave, often even hiding it from themselves by "forgetting" it. This "forgetting" might be conscious, or it might be unconscious. It might be an intentional "forgetting", or it might be that their internal system has covered it up in order to protect them, in order that they don't have to remember and think about it every day of their lives.

For some others, the memory or details of the abuse might come out much later in life. Perhaps they have been triggered right back into the memory by a current situation, or perhaps they have finally realised that what happened Was. Not. OK.

So many people who have endured some sort of sexual trauma will say "Oh, it wasn't that bad", or "but I'm sure I had a part to play in it, it was partially my fault", or "it was my fault", or "I should have known better". Some might say "but I felt physical arousal during it, so therefore I must have had a part to play" or "but I really wanted the attention – it must have been my fault". Some people say "it wasn't sexual abuse, I wasn't raped".

Sometimes people are so convinced that it was their fault, or that they had some part to play in it, that they feel too ashamed to even talk about it. Sometimes the shame, or overwhelm of other feelings around the incident (or incidents), is so overwhelming that they have blocked off the memory altogether and, as a form of self-protection, have either consciously or unconsciously chosen to forget about it.

Two things are happening here.

One: there is a gross misunderstanding about what constitutes sexual abuse and sexual assault, and this contributes to the confusion felt by the sufferer.

Two: when we have suffered some sort of sexual trauma, we more often than not feel as though we have had a part to play in it and that it is therefore our fault. No matter if were two, three, five, nine, eleven, or adult.

Sexual trauma is never our fault. No sexual trauma is ever our fault.

Another way of defining sexual trauma is that of any sexually based experience that leaves us feeling "icky", disgust, fear, or shame. In other words, any sexually oriented act that leaves us with a horrible feeling – even an unwanted or uncomfortable sexual experience. And yes, this can happen in romantic relationships too.

Sexual trauma is never our fault. No sexual trauma is ever our fault.

All childhood experiences of sexual trauma result in a feeling of "icky" because, as children, we do not have the emotional maturity to process anything of a sexual nature. This sexually based experience can be anything from "grooming" – being the centre of attention by the abuser – to a kiss, right through to oral, anal or vaginal touching or penetration, and / or rape. But we will come on to childhood sexual trauma – generally more referred to as childhood sexual abuse – in a moment.

Rape and consent

Another area where people who have suffered sexual trauma are often stuck, or confused, is around the area of consent. The notion of consent becomes mixed up with feelings of guilt, shame or fear.

In 2015, Thames Valley Police made a powerful video around the topic of rape and consent – you can find it on YouTube, just put in "cup of tea consent" and it will come up. They say the law is very clear: "if the sex is non-consensual, then it is rape".

Their video talks about consent – and tea. If you offer someone a cup of tea, and they say yes, then great, make them a cup of tea. They might have changed their mind once the tea is made – and you might find it annoying that they have changed their mind. But for heaven's sake, don't pour tea down their throat when they don't want it. Just leave the cup of tea. Oh yes, and by the way, unconscious people don't drink tea.

Sometimes the victims of rape are in a state of "freeze" when an act of a sexual nature is occurring, and they cannot protest.

This does not make it consensual. If someone doesn't notice that the person they are engaged in a sexual activity with has frozen, then what does it say about that person engaged in the act?

In the past, we might have heard someone say "Oh, but she was wearing a short skirt, and she was asking for it", for example. No. Wearing a short skirt and wanting to look feminine is not giving consent for a sexual attack.

We might also hear "Oh, but he got so drunk, he was asking for it". No. People are permitted to drink if they so wish, without worrying that their bodies might be taken advantage of when their defences are down as a result of alcohol.

All sexual abuse is non-consensual

The Metropolitan Police's video is around the notion of rape and consent, and it is a very, very important video. But other types of sexual assault that do not include rape are actually non-consensual too.

Seeking help

Many people do not consider their sexual abuse to be "bad enough" to seek help. This applies to people who are raped, and to those who suffer alternative types of sexual assault, or sexual trauma. Please seek help. When we are sexually abused or assaulted in any way, it affects our psyche. And if we keep this buried inside, then it will dictate how we feel about ourselves and about our lives, and it will significantly diminish our life experience.

There is help out there for anyone who has suffered any type of sexual trauma. But, I know, it can feel very difficult to come forward and ask for that help.

Did it really happen? Was it really that bad?

Very often, survivors of any type of sexual assault and abuse will ask themselves the question "did this really happen?". This is so common and true whether the trauma occurred in childhood or in adulthood. Sometimes too, a survivor might ask themselves the question "was it really that bad?". This line of internal questioning can continue throughout treatment too, and it can reoccur even after we begin to heal. If this is happening for you, please know it this is entirely normal and that there is nothing wrong with you for having these thoughts.

Reasons why survivors question the abuse or its validity will vary from person to person. It can be due to the feeling of toxic shame carried by the victim which makes them feel they are to blame. It could also be the body's way of trying to protect itself from the hideous nature of the crime. And it can also be due to the unsupportive nature of the environment at the time, and this will be referred to again, later on in this chapter and in Chapter 9.

Any type of sexual trauma is an extreme violation of an individual's boundaries and will have dire consequences on how that individual will view themselves and the world as a result. And this extreme violation can often result in us questioning whether the abuse actually happened. But the body never lies. The body tells us that the abuse occurred, even if the mind is questioning it.

Children and sexual abuse

Very, very sadly, sexual abuse of children is off the scale in its magnitude. Sexual abusers of children are very often people that the children know and trust, too. This might be a parent, an adult family member, an older sibling or cousin, a teacher, or a family friend. Very often – but not always – it happens behind closed doors. Sometimes the child will know that it is wrong – they will sense it – but being a child, they will not have the resources to do anything about it. And the abuse will continue. Sometimes the child is told to not tell anyone, and it feels too frightening for the child to go against these orders from someone in a position of power, so they keep quiet.

I am yet to meet anyone who has suffered a sexual trauma – either in childhood or adulthood – who is not suffering as a result.

For many people who suffer sexual abuse, there is a secret that comes with it. The abuse was either hidden by the sufferer or it was ignored or shushed by others. In the past, in a heart-breaking number of cases, childhood sexual abuse was not taken seriously enough by those purporting to care for the child.

I thought it might be useful here to add an account of a childhood sexual abuse survivor. She has, of course, given her full permission for it to be published here. She first talks about the abuse and how she felt at the time, and then she recounts it after she has been through trauma therapy and found some recovery.

I include this case study because it gives us such a deep insight into what it really feels like for a child to go through this. Her name has been changed for confidentiality reasons.

Tanya's story

When I was growing up, I was really good at drama, and one of the drama teachers at my school favoured me over the other children. I was at boarding school from the age of eight, so I spent a lot of time at school. The drama teacher used to bring me chocolates and flowers regularly, and I would share them with my friends. I loved the attention, loved it, and even though occasionally I'd get the feeling of "weird", "icky", or even "panic" around the attention he gave me, I pushed those feelings away, because being the favourite and being the one who got the chocolates and the flowers, when no-one else did, felt really important to me. It filled me up and made me feel special. I never let on how much I loved the attention though, it felt a bit weird to me, and I didn't think anyone would understand, so I kept quiet about that. I was 10 years old.

Over the next two years, the chocolates and flowers were pretty much weekly. I knew the days he was in school and the days he was not. He wore strong aftershave, and the smell of it used to saturate the drama rooms, and it gave me comfort because it was his. I wasn't pretty or popular, but I was good at drama, and this teacher adored me. His attention towards me fuelled me, it kept me going – it drove me. After a while, I craved it, and I started to miss him on the days he wasn't at school. I felt sad when he wasn't there; his attention filled me up and made me happy, and I had a hole inside me any days that he didn't come to the school. I was 10 years old. Then I was 11 years old. Then I was 12 years old, and this all continued. My feelings towards him became stronger every year. On the day I left the school, when I was 12 years old, he kissed me on the mouth outside the art room.

I can't remember details of the kiss, but I think he asked me first, because I do remember that I wanted it to happen, I wanted it so badly. But the moment it happened – I hated it. After he'd kissed me, he said "If you were 16, I'd do other things to you". I suddenly felt so scared even though I didn't really know why; I had this overwhelming sense that I'd done something terribly, terribly wrong and very, very bad. I felt like my insides had imploded, and I wasn't in my body anymore, I wasn't anywhere. I ran away from the art room and found my parents who had been looking for me, ready to take me home for the summer holidays. I remember them saying "Oh, there you are. We've been looking for you". I didn't say a word in response; I couldn't have spoken if I had tried. I remember sitting quietly in the back of the car, as we drove away from the school towards home, desperately trying to appear normal even though my insides were vacuous and trembling at the same time. I couldn't think. I didn't know what to do with myself. I was stunned, frozen, baffled. I couldn't make sense of it – because I'd wanted it so much – then, when it had happened, I hadn't wanted it at all, and I couldn't understand how those two could coexist. I was so desperately confused. I couldn't contemplate it all. It made me want to curl up in a ball and not be seen. I felt dirty, I felt disgusting. I felt bad. I was a bad person. I was the worst person that had ever existed in the history of the world. I couldn't tell my parents; they would hate me and look at me with disgust and see me for the terrible person that I was. I was all alone with this. I felt like I wanted to die. I don't remember that summer holiday at all. I had begun to properly shut down.

The next term, I was at senior school. A couple of weeks into the new school, I received an envelope with a bump in it meaning something extra was in it. I recognised the writing. I knew it was from him. It smelt like him. I could smell his aftershave. I went into overwhelming panic. I couldn't even hold the envelope, let alone open it and read the letter. A fellow pupil saw my distress and took me, carrying the envelope herself, to the housemistress. I couldn't speak. I was frozen. I was crying, but I couldn't find any words. The housemistress opened the letter and saw some of the words "I love you", "I miss you", "you are the best thing that ever happened to me…" but I couldn't read any more. The bump in the envelope turned out to be a bracelet. I was 12. He was 55. I remember speaking to my mother on the phone from my housemistress's office, and I remember her saying "you won't hear from him again". And that was the end of it.

At the age of 18, I went back to work at the school, for the Christmas term, at the behest of my parents – I was told that it was a good way to get some pocket money for a gap year. I avoided the drama rooms, but I remember spotting him across the playground one time... What I saw was a broken man, and all I could think to myself was "I did that, I broke him, it's all my fault. I'm a terrible, terrible person".

This is another version of what happened, as written by Tanya at the age of 43, having done some years of trauma work, and with a pretty thorough understanding, at last, of what she went through and the impact that it had had on her:

When I was 10 years old, I was groomed by a 55-year-old drama teacher at school for two years. He sexually abused me, and the last time I ever saw him – when I was 12 – he kissed me on the mouth and told me that, if I was 16, he would do other things to me; he was 55, I was 12. I turned in on myself, gripped with shame to my core. His interest in me was discovered a few months later, and I was told I wouldn't be hearing from him again, but that was it. The following year, I started playing around with food and eating less – great for hiding, or so I thought, and within a year anorexia had taken a hold. But then, when I was 15, I was "found out" with my anorexia, so after treatment, where I pretended I wanted to get well even when I didn't, I took to drugs in secret. When I was 18, and went back to that same prep school to work there for a term, I didn't eat for the entire term. I didn't know why I wasn't eating, but I did remember comments from 12-year-old pupils like "you're really thin", and "why don't you eat?" – but their comments confused me, because I couldn't see any other option than to not eat. Looking back, I can see how me going to work there for a term was like putting a sheep back among the wolves, even though I didn't realise how unwell I was, but it never once occurred to me that I didn't need to feel like that. I had a low-level anxiety, a low-level terror really, and it was so "normal" for me that I didn't know things could be any different. I was too gripped with shame, self-disgust and self-hatred to say "no I won't go back there" when the job was offered.

After this term, and into my early twenties, I became a drug addict and an alcoholic, a compulsive eater too. I would grab at anything external from the moment I woke to the moment I went to sleep – but I was OK at getting on with everyday life for a while. Well, until I was 28, I guess, because by then all I was doing was eating cocaine and drinking absinthe, not knowing night from day. This lasted for three years. I got clean and sober at 31. I had a job (even though I didn't like the job). I even got married and had my first child, but I felt so far removed from other people that I was just convinced I was odd, or that there was something fundamentally wrong with me. I hated sex, and I needed to feel extremely skinny in order to be naked with a man. Did I feel as though there was much wrong with my life? Not really, I just thought I was a bit odd, a bit disconnected, and a bit lost – but I thought it was my fault and that I had just been born "wrong". I knew that I wanted to feel safe – I thought material safety would help this (it did for a while) – and I would constantly seek external things to help me gain a sense of safety. I chose messing around with food so that I could stay very slim – there was something in the safety in being skinny that helped me not to feel too many emotions – smoking cigarettes, shopping, lovely haircuts... I didn't do any of these to excess at all, I could afford them all, and I didn't think they were problematic at the time either. On paper, they were not at all. I wasn't anorexic anymore, I wasn't overspending on clothes, I wasn't overspending on haircuts, I wasn't smoking so much I had a smoker's cough. I realise now that it wasn't about "what" I was doing, it was about the reasons why I was doing those things. I needed to stay slim so I didn't have to feel my real feelings (I had no idea what they even were). I needed to look good on the outside so that no-one would see the real me, the broken, permanently damaged me that I was so utterly ashamed of. I needed to have a healthy bank balance. I needed all these things *because they made me feel a sense of safety.* I can tell you now that I had absolutely no concept of the feeling of "feeling safe inside", "feeling safe in my own skin"; if you'd mentioned that to me, I would have felt rather confused, and probably also would have felt a bit ashamed that I couldn't feel that, as though that just confirmed the fact that there was something fundamentally wrong with me.

Layer by layer, with the help of EMDR and analytical hypnotherapy, over a three-year period, I managed to chisel away at this drama teacher incident. It took a long time. This wasn't rape, this wasn't some sort of hideous sexual intercourse assault with a small child – I didn't even think it was sexual abuse at first. *Yet it took me many, many sessions of intensive trauma therapy before I could properly talk about it and before I could even say his name out loud.* What was the primary thing that took me so long to heal from? It was shame.

Shame. Shame. Shame.

I had felt monumental shame around wanting all that attention in the first place, and monumental shame around the fact that I had thought I had loved him. I had felt tremendous guilt that I had dobbed him in when he sent me a necklace a few months later; I believed I had led him on. I was wracked with guilt and shame around the whole event and, although I had absolutely no idea what "shame" was at the time, I felt as though on a fundamental level there was something terribly wrong with me. I now understand completely that this was a deep feeling of toxic shame. I thought I had been born "wrong". I had wanted his attention – I had wanted him, then I hadn't wanted it when it had happened, therefore I was very, very, very bad. I had led him on, and it was all my fault.

Only now, after all those years of trauma therapy, do I understand that I was a powerless, underage child, taken advantage of sexually by a middle-aged man.

They call these men paedophiles, and he should, I now understand, have been arrested.

When Tanya began her trauma work and had started to describe what had happened to her, she didn't understand that this was a type of sexual abuse – she could not find it in herself to understand that she wasn't to blame. She challenged endlessly any education on sexual abuse, finding nooks and crannies in which her view of this being "non-sexual abuse" could remain. The reason she did this was because her feelings of "I am wrong", "I am permanently damaged", "I am bad", "I am disgusting" were so intense, so deep, and felt so fundamentally part of her core, that she simply couldn't believe, for one moment, that it might not have been her fault and that she didn't have to feel this way.

Tanya is not alone. Almost every person I have spoken to who has some sexual trauma has thought and felt – deeply – that they had a part to play in the abuse.

Almost every single one.

And this is largely, in part, due to the feeling of toxic shame that we talked about in Chapter 5. The impact of toxic shame and the transfer of shame are such important concepts for us to learn when we are healing from sexual trauma. Here is a quick reminder.

Sexual abuse, of any description, is a shameful act on the part of the perpetrator. But perpetrators don't own their shame – otherwise they wouldn't be taking advantage of people (adults or children) sexually in the first place. They don't have any healthy shame around sexual abuse. Therefore, the shame of the shameful act – the shame that is in the ether because it is a shameful act – is transferred to the victim as toxic shame. And the victim feels like it is their own shame. As though it is all their fault. The victim feels bad, dirty, shameful, disgusting, worthless, unlovable, and often responsible. The victim has taken on the toxic shame that actually belongs to the abuser.

Other effects of sexual abuse

Sexual trauma can affect us, as mentioned earlier, in ways that one cannot even imagine if one has not had sexual trauma. Along with the host of negative self-beliefs that will ensue, other after-effects can include: blocks to creativity, relationship difficulties, sexual behaviours which might be promiscuous or starved (sexual anorexia), a hatred and deep fear around sex, body hatred, an inability to conceive, an inability to have healthy relationships with others (men or women), loss of sense of self, feelings of derealisation, feelings of not being present in the world, eating disorders, addictions, self-harm, depression, anxiety, suicidal ideation and suicide itself.

But there are other factors to consider around sexual abuse too, over and above the actual abuse itself. The abuse is bad enough, but our environment at the time, and after the event, will also contribute to our handling of the abuse. Our environment, at the time of any abuse, is absolutely key in how we might get through it, and how much unresolved trauma we might consequently be left with in our systems.

Our environment at the time of the abuse

If we think back to Tanya's story, we will recall that she felt she had to stay quiet. She did not feel safe enough to talk about what happened and how it had made her feel. A part of this was the toxic shame that she was experiencing, the shame that her abuser could not own himself. But another part of her fear of speaking up was related to her lack of a secure enough environment – as perceived by her internal world – where she could have felt OK enough to talk about what had happened.

So many adult survivors of childhood sexual abuse do not feel they are able to tell another adult about the abuse, either at the time or afterwards. And some who do report the abuse are still not able to fully explain how it has made them feel, nor able to fully process it. Survivors of adult sexual abuse often experience exactly the same.

So much of this is due to shame. Societal shame, familial shame, and the shame felt by the victim. But so much of this too, is the absence of a secure enough environment in which the victim feels safe enough to share their story.

There is a societal taboo around sexual abuse. When sexual abuse is mentioned, we, as the listener, will pick up on the feeling of shame around the shameful act, and we often cannot cope with this feeling ourselves. This will happen even if we are hearing about the abuse third hand – in other words, when we are hearing about it happen to someone else. So, we don't want to talk about it. We are not able to handle the enormity of sexual trauma and its impact, so we prefer to bury it under the carpet, believing that this will help the victim in the same way we think it is helping us. We often do not have the inner resources to feel able to face or confront such a shameful act. And victims pick up on this. Victims of sexual trauma already feel shame. And if the environment cannot handle the feeling of shame, sexual trauma victims will continue to stay silent *because their silence will feel like a safer place to be.*

In order to help people to come forward about their sexual trauma, we need to provide a shame-free, understanding, emotional holding space that is big enough to be able to hold all of that toxic shame that the victim is experiencing. The victim needs to know on a cellular level – with every cell in their body – that it is safe to talk about their experience and that, by doing so, they will feel relief. If there is any chance that their system detects a threat to this sense of safety, they will not speak; it simply won't feel safe enough.

Vulnerability and the victim

Many children who suffer any type of sexual trauma are already in an emotionally vulnerable position before the abuse even occurs. That is to say, their inner experience of external relationships is already lacking in its core connection strength.

This means that there is a developmental deficit already existing in the child (remember Chapter 1 when we talked about the lack of the 4 Ss leaving a developmental deficit inside us).

When we have a developmental deficit as a child, we will do anything in our power, unconsciously, in order to get this need met. This is not dissimilar to a starving child who will do almost anything to get hold of food including going through bins full of faeces in case there is a scrap to be found in there, because they are so hungry. Seeking to get our needs met, when we are a child, is a largely systemic action. We unconsciously feel drawn to anything that might meet our needs. In the case of sexual abuse, a child is, on one level, unconsciously seeking to have an unmet need met. This does not mean, of course, that they are asking to be taken advantage of – good God no. But it does mean that their system is seeking to get its needs met in any which way is available to them, in order to attain the sense of connection that every child needs. And if the only means of connection is through an abuser, then a child will most probably take it. They simply are not emotionally, physically or cognitively developed enough to be able to do any different. And having this need for connection met through the abuse, will only further compound a victim's feelings of confusion around the event.

Children who are taken advantage of sexually by older predators will generally have a "need bank" that is already desperately low. Somehow, paedophiles and predators can detect this when they choose their victims.

Having an absence of those 4 Ss, and consequent developmental deficits, does not automatically lead to sexual abuse. But a child who is sexually abused will almost definitely have a depleted need bank before the abuse even takes place.

And this leads us on to the next chapter "Where was Mum and where were the grown-ups?".

CHAPTER 9

Where was Mum and where were the grown-ups?

"The attachment between mother and child is the deepest form of nurture that exists, and the most painful of all wounds when it is disrupted."
— Ana Isabel, Analytical Hypnotherapist

It's an old therapeutic cliché isn't it: "it's all about my mother". People are a bit tired of hearing that phrase now, especially as we advance in our understanding around the human psyche.

But the truth is, there is some wisdom in that old cliché, even if we have moved on in our sophistication around understanding what and why. And this deep-dive into that wisdom is helpful to understand, in order to help us in our healing process.

It is all about our parents, too. Both of them. And other adults in our lives when we are children. The supposed grown-ups. Let's take a look.

Big T trauma and Mum

What has become evident, during the years that I have been witnessing people heal, is that when there is a substantial traumatic event, or a "Big T" trauma, during childhood, there is always an attachment story that goes with it. Whether the trauma is sexual abuse, physical abuse, school abuse, or substantial peer conflict (for example bullying), once we have targeted that trauma in sessions and processed it, almost every single client afterwards arrives at the question:

"But where was Mum?", "How could Mum have allowed this to happen?".

And very often, this is the part of the healing that takes the longest. This is often the most painful part of the wound for us to come to terms with and, in some cases, the most difficult for us to access.

When Tanya (from the last chapter) was in therapy, the sexual abuse from the drama teacher was targeted directly. Processing the abuse felt difficult. Painful. But as soon as the worst of it was processed and left in the past, what remained was the harsh reality that her mother had not stood up for her at the time. And this was actually the wound that Tanya found to be the deepest and the most painful of all – even compared with the sexual trauma itself. It took many more sessions, over a period of time, for Tanya to be able to connect with the gravity and the loss that she felt, knowing Mum had not done enough at the time, and for this next stage of Tanya's healing jigsaw to take shape. And this is the case for many adult survivors of childhood physical, sexual or emotional traumas.

To heal these core wounds, we generally find ourselves going back to the primal attachment figure, which is most often Mum. And we allow our system to process and metabolise the fact that our mum simply had not done enough to help us at the time. In the case of Tanya, as an adult, she was logically able to see that things were different in those days: sexual trauma was not taken seriously back when it had happened to her, and people were much less aware of the impact that this type of abuse could have on people in those days. Tanya understood this in her head. But her system, her physiological network of threat detection and trauma response, did not possess that logic when she was younger. And nor should it have – our needs as a child are not able to accommodate an outdated belief system that happens to be a part of our parents' story.

Ben came for trauma healing at 25-years-old. He had been bullied at school. He had repeatedly been ganged up on by another group of boys, during term time and out of school during the holidays, from the age of seven. He processed the bullying from his peers relatively quickly in the sessions, but then he too was left with the earth-shattering realisation "Mum didn't stop this". Mum had known about the bullying at the time, as had the school, but the school had told Mum that they had it under control, and Mum had believed the school. When Ben's internal system realised and properly experienced how it felt not to have received enough support from Mum, he was aghast. We spent a few sessions processing his disbelief, his anger, and then finally his sense of loss for what he could have had in terms of support from his mum, that he had not received. He came through it, but it was painful, messy and deeply emotional work. Interestingly, his father was just as complicit in knowing about and not putting a stop to the bullying, but

Ben's system was yearning for Mum to have been the one to have sorted it out, not Dad.

Sofia, 23, had dyslexia and dyspraxia, which hadn't been recognised until she was nine years old. She had felt stupid at school, and this feeling of "I am stupid" continued with her into her adulthood. This negative belief took her right back to being in the classroom, aged eight. A stern teacher was calling her stupid. She desensitised the feelings towards her teacher, and the other children in the classroom, relatively quickly. She processed this scene until the younger Sofia was able to see that the problem actually lay with the school not spotting her learning differences, and that of course she was not stupid. But even after we had processed this successfully, even after she realised during the processing "I am not stupid, it was the school that was not noticing nor accommodating my processing needs adequately enough", her system then raised the question "but how did Mum let me down so badly that she didn't see this was happening to me?". And this absence of unconditional support from her mum was an even deeper wound for Sofia to face. It came with the beliefs "I am not worth it, I'm not worth it to my mum, I'm not good enough as a person, I am not worthy of love". And with those beliefs too, came deep feelings of shame. Sofia had to face and process all of this too, before she could fully leave the bullying in the background. Her mother had simply not been emotionally available enough to be able to see that her daughter was struggling at school. With Sofia, as with Ben, her dad was also emotionally unavailable, and did not spot his daughter's distress at school. Yet during the healing sessions, Sofia's system was yearning for Mum to have done something, not Dad, just like Ben's.

Jodie came to me in her thirties. She had been physically abused by Dad all through her early years. Dad would hit her, shame her, tell her she was useless – it was really horrible, overt abuse. It was horrific for her to have to recall the horror of the abuse from Dad, horrific. But she came through it, and she processed it. But what took more sessions, and actually longer for Jodie to come to terms with within her internal system, within her inner child psyche, was the question "where was Mum?", "how could Mum have allowed this to happen?", "why did Mum allow Dad to hit me and shame me?", "what was wrong with me that Mum didn't take me away and keep me safe?". Before trauma therapy, it had not occurred to Jodie that she had yearned for Mum to have done something at the time. But as she began to heal and do the inner work, her internal system experienced an enormous sense of loss that Mum had not intervened. She did come to terms with this eventually, but it was difficult and painful work.

Some children, in the UK especially, are sent to boarding school for their education, as I have mentioned before. Lots of adults who went to boarding school and suffered hideous trauma while there, come for trauma work later in life; this is most prominent in those who started boarding from seven or eight years old, but also older. We process the beatings, the canings, the bulling from pupils and teachers, and the homesickness. But the worst part of all, for almost everyone who suffered during their boarding school years, is again when they reach a point in the healing at which their internal system asks the question "why did Mum let this happen?". "Why did Mum send me away to school so young?". "Where was Mum?". Again, Dad will have been just as complicit in the decision to send their child to boarding school; but in the healing sessions our system asks "but where was Mum?".

Many, many people wanting help with childhood abuse (physical, emotional or sexual) from another significant adult or person, process the abuse first. But next, almost always, the deepest innermost part of their system asks the question "but where was Mum?".

"Where was Mum?", "how did Mum allow this to happen?", "why couldn't Mum see what was happening?", "why didn't Mum stop this?", "why did Mum send me into this environment?" are the types of questions that our inner, wounded child suffers from most profoundly.

Why the emphasis on Mum?

So why is there such an emphasis on Mum? Why is it that our systems connect so deeply to a need for Mum to have been the one to help? Why does our system have that yearning for Mum to have behaved differently much, much more often than it comes back to needing Dad, regardless of what Dad might or might not have done, or how complicit he might have been?

The exact answer to this question is up for debate, if there even is an exact answer. But there are some simple pointers that probably contribute to our younger psyche feeling so reliant on Mum as the primary caregiver, safety net and main "sorter" of life – and conversely, for those reasons, she will be the first one to be "blamed" internally, for not being available enough, by the youngster. And these pointers are worth knowing about, and considering, at least, especially if we wish to heal from these wounds and properly move on from them.

Let's take a look.

Mum as the primary carer

Traditionally, mums have been the nurturing figure for a child and have been the parent who spends more time with the child. This is indeed changing. Dads are staying at home to look after children now, much more than in the past, and in some cases, children are being raised by two dads without a mother. It will be fascinating to see how research findings on the importance of a mother are impacted by this different, emerging dynamic. There are reports coming through already, from children who are now in their twenties, who have been raised by two dads, and they do comment on how much they grieve the loss of a mother figure. But there might also be other stories of children raised by two dads who do not feel the loss of the mother figure. We will have to see.

But back to Mum. We are carried in the womb for months by our mum. We are birthed by Mum. We are gazed at by Mum. There is skin-to-skin contact – from Mum. We are breastfed, if possible, by Mum. All of these experiences with Mum contribute to how our neural pathways wire in the brain. If Mum is emotionally present, loving, safe, joyful, authentic, emotionally robust, gentle, kind, tactile, compassionate and understanding enough – then we will have a pretty good chance of developing into fully functioning, emotionally whole adults. But when Mum is lacking significantly enough in any of those areas, because she is still carrying her own unresolved trauma and is not able to give us what we need, then we will feel it, and our neural pathways will wire accordingly.

The first 1000 days of life

The first 1000 days of any child's life are extraordinarily important. This is not talked about enough in the mainstream, but it is now fully recognised at a government level in both the US and the UK.

The first 1000 days of life – *from conception* – we now know are some of the most critical for a child in terms of how the neural networks in the brain begin to be formed and wired. In other words, those first 1000 days are the time during which a child begins to make the internal decisions about themselves and about the world. And of course, that time is spent predominantly with Mum.

And the first 270 (or thereabouts) days are spent in the womb of the mother. We simply can't get any closer to our mum than that.

In the womb

When we are in the womb, we pick up on an awful lot of emotion that our mother is feeling. Our mother's right brain is directly and physically linked to the placenta of the foetus – whereas her left brain is not.

Miranda, 26, had suffered panic attacks for years. After

successful sessions on her anxiety, she wanted to work on her fear of the London Underground trains. I asked her to imagine her worst-case scenario, and she described the terror of seeing the escalator at her local Tube station. Her feelings of being trapped, helpless and powerless were extremely high, and she felt it physically – or somatically – throughout her body. She believed "I can't do this", "I can't stand it". We dropped back in time, and she found herself in the womb. As she processed, she realised that the terror she was feeling, when she had found herself in the womb, actually belonged to her mum. Mum had been told that Miranda was going to be a sick baby once born, and this had been terrifying her mother in the final weeks of the pregnancy. I checked in with Miranda and asked "But were you born sick?" To which she responded "No, I was really healthy". So we had a doctor come in, in Miranda's imagination, and the doctor told Mum that her baby was going to be fine. As Miranda imagined all of this taking place during the session, during the processing, she was able to release all of Mum's anxiety until she felt ready to be born. Miranda then reimagined her birth, to a non-anxious mum. And her fear of Underground trains has since disappeared.

Maria found herself back in the womb in the session too, and just knew that she really, really didn't want to be born. She felt panicked and fearful about entering into the world. She didn't understand why. Mum hadn't been particularly anxious, and her family unit was relatively stable. But as we processed her experience as a foetus, what emerged was that Mum had been holding on to a whole heap of unresolved grief from her own childhood, and Maria had unknowingly picked up on this in the womb. Before she felt safe enough to be reborn, she needed to grieve Mum's childhood, along with the impact that Mum's unresolved trauma had had on her, before she felt ready to be born. She cried and cried, as she released all of her mother's unprocessed loss that had lodged inside her whilst she was a foetus. Once she was ready, Maria was reborn feeling OK and as though she wanted to be a part of life.

Alex didn't want to be born, because he knew that, once he was born, his mother wouldn't connect with him. He had picked up on his mother's own lack of feeling safe, while he was in the womb, and it had made him feel unsafe as a result – not safe enough to be born. He had preverbal memories of being in a cot too, trying to get Mum's attention, but Mum was always looking away, unable to connect. He processed all of this, and also did some work on Mum (in his imagination), to get Mum feeling more secure around having a baby and being able to connect with it – and only then did he feel safe enough to be reborn in the session.

These case studies, and many more like them, really do demonstrate how babies in the womb directly experience the emotions of the mother. These can be either buried or accessible emotions, or both. When we are in the womb, we take on Mum's feelings as if they are our own. With this direct physical link to Mum's emotions, adrenalin and hormones, it's no wonder that we respond to how Mum is feeling. We have no way of differentiating, in the womb, what Mum is feeling versus what we are feeling.

Infancy and early toddlerhood

"Children are not resilient, they are malleable."

– Allan Schore

It has long been believed, and widely discussed, that children are resilient. And children can certainly learn resilience, but, as Allan Schore perfectly states above, children are actually malleable before they are resilient. This is absolutely true during those first 1000 days of life, from infancy into the start of toddlerhood, and I certainly agree with Allan Schore that babies and toddlers are malleable rather than resilient. So, what is the difference between resilience and malleability?

To be resilient implies a sense of agency. It implies a sense of understanding behind the perceived ability to adapt. And as young children, we can certainly learn resilience, especially if we are shown those 4 Ss enough of the time during our childhood.

But infants and toddlers are not necessarily old enough to learn resilience, because they have no sense of agency. And, as you might remember from Chapter 3, infants and toddlers have no left-brain function just yet. With their young brains at the height of neuroplasticity, and with such a direct right-brain connection with Mum, in addition to the immaturity of their left brain, it is actually much more fitting to say that infants and toddlers are malleable.

They might appear resilient, because they appear to be adapting. But this type of adapting is malleability and so often at the baby's peril if the relationship with the caregiver is not safe enough. But infants and toddlers are powerless to change this.

With Mum as our entry point into the world, before we learn to speak and experience our own thoughts via our left brain, we rely on her as the chief interpreter for all that is going on around us.

The importance of "co-regulation" for the infant and toddler

As infants and toddlers, we completely rely on Mum to "co-regulate" our emotions. We are simply not able to do this ourselves. This means that when we are stressed, and our difficult emotions become heightened, we need Mum to soothe us. When we feel joy, we need Mum to mirror that back to us too. We need this upregulation and downregulation to be occurring with Mum, because we can't do it on our own yet. We haven't learned how.

Our primary source of connection between us and the outside world is through our connection and co-regulation with Mum.

Forty years or so ago, John Bowlby developed his acclaimed "attachment theory". It was brilliant – he worked out different "styles" of attachment between a child and their primary caregiver (usually Mum), based on the child's behaviours around and without Mum. Bowlby's attachment theory is used by many people, as we try to work out our attachment style and what that means for how we might feel and behave in relationships as adults.

What we are learning more and more, however, is the need to study emotion, rather than focussing solely on behaviour. Bowlby's attachment theory studied a child's *behaviour* and worked out attachment styles given a child's behaviour around Mum. Although this was a groundbreaking discovery, the studies of the infant and toddler internal systems have been even more closely scrutinised and researched since then.

We now understand, thanks to MRI scanners and a lot of research, that we need to be studying the *emotional* connection and *emotional* regulation between the mother and the child, in addition to looking at the behaviour.

During those first 1000 days of our life, from conception through to toddlerhood, we learn how to regulate our emotions and whether it is safe to connect in the world or not. *And we learn this primarily through Mum.*

If Mum is dysregulated through being depressed, taking substances, feeling anxious, unsure, or feeling shut down or cut off from herself and / or the world, or if Mum has any unresolved trauma, then as a baby we will feel all of those experiences too. These experiences of Mum's will influence the picture of our own internal world that we paint based on the internal and external world of Mum.

Connection and safety

Another way we can think about the co-regulation and connection that we need during those first 1000 days is by remembering those 4 Ss that we have talked about before:

Seen, Soothed, Safe and Secure.

As a baby, we need to feel *at a cellular level* – because we are right-brained when we are that young – that we are seen, soothed, safe and secure, enough of the time. And for a mother to be able to provide that for us, she ideally needs to have resolved a good proportion of her own trauma, in order that she is able to meet her own internal 4 Ss. We mentioned this in Chapter 4.

Yet very few of us receive this cellular level, felt sense, of being seen, of safety, of soothing and security, enough of the time. And as a result, many, many children have grown into adulthood with at least some unresolved trauma from this time period. Not because Mum has been "bad", but because Mum was still blocked off from experiencing her own self, her own sense of self-safety, and her own ability to self-soothe – potentially even her own ability to properly see herself, while she was raising her child.

So perhaps, when we realise the science behind the mother-baby connection and the importance of the connection that we have in the womb to Mum's right brain, we can pretty much see why it could be largely all about our mothers – in a very, very deep way.

Sometimes, as adults, with all of our self-protective layers in place to prevent us from feeling our deep, emotional pain, we might look back at our childhood and notice, thanks to our fully developed prefrontal cortex that makes adult, rational analyses of situations, that Mum was doing her best. And sometimes, with this knowledge as an adult, this rationalisation can prevent us from really getting into the deep, emotional wounds that we have been covering up.

Even though we can probably look back now, as adults, on our experiences with Mum with reasoning and logic, if we didn't receive those 4 Ss enough at the time then our felt experience around mum during our childhoods will have been very different to what our adult brain can understand looking back. And when that felt experience at the time is too much for our system to process, then there is a high chance we will have feelings of anxiety, feelings of sadness, and any other difficult feelings too, just buried pretty deeply.

It is very difficult for us, if not impossible, during those 1000 days of life before our left brain comes online, to differentiate between what is Mum's stuff and what is our stuff. We often carry both experiences, unprocessed, right on into our adult lives.

And those first 1000 days set us up for our whole childhood – and into adulthood.

If those first 1000 days are secure, co-regulated, connected in a loving way, and if they feel safe, then we will probably thrive. If there is a disruption to co-regulation and a sense of safety, however, unless addressed later on in childhood, this disruption will be our foundation and will continue into adulthood too.

Early childhood

This need for our 4 Ss from our caregivers does not stop at toddlerhood. We need this level of care all the way through our childhood. Our brain networks continue to develop and grow and form connections all through our young lives. Very often during trauma work, when we are taken back to the core trauma, we land somewhere between the ages of conception and the age of seven, eight, or nine. It's amazing how much unresolved material we accumulate in our systems up until that age.

The significance of the ages of seven, eight and nine

We might have heard about the age of seven, eight or nine being significant in a child's life. This is because at around this age, our left-brain, or our prefrontal cortex, has a huge growth spurt. It is coming online gradually before that, but at the seven, eight or nine year mark it is much more involved.

When we reach this milestone, our left-brain becomes more independently engaged throughout our day. We form cohesive thoughts about ourselves and about our lives. From this age onwards, our need for the parent to be the sole rationaliser begins, slowly, to diminish.

However, whatever we have learned about ourselves and the world preceding this age will be pretty much set in stone by now. Therefore, whatever we have picked up and sensed before now, we will give thought to via our pre-frontal cortex. And once we start to properly think about all of the messages that we have received before this age, about ourselves and about the world, these neural connections will stick.

If we have learned, before now, that we are enough, we are loved and that the world is a safe place, then those neural networks will strengthen.

But if we have learned that we are not enough, we are not lovable, and that the world is not a safe place, then these ideas will strengthen as neural connections instead.

Our brain, around this age, also becomes less elastic – less prone to persuasion and quick neural pathway correction. What this means is that whatever we have learned already, properly solidifies.

Those first seven, eight or nine years of life are absolutely critical in how our neural pathways connect and program information, both about ourselves, and about the world. And once we reach this age, whatever we have learned before this, will stick.

A tonne of wet cement

Even after the age of seven, eight or nine, however, the words of our parents will continue to affect us. And this can have some very dramatic, and dire, consequences too.

Let's think back to Tanya from the last chapter, who had sexual trauma as a result of the behaviour of her drama teacher between the ages of nine and 12 years old.

It took a long, long, long time – even in trauma therapy – for Tanya to fully understand that this grooming and kiss from the teacher was not her fault.

When Tanya was asked "If it had happened to someone else instead of you, then would it be their fault that it had happened?", she was able to respond with "categorically no, it would not be their fault". But when it came to whether the teacher kissing her was her fault or not, she was adamant that she was different and that this was absolutely her doing and that she was to blame. She found it impossible for a long, long time to shift from the notion that she had had a part to play in the abuse.

Then one day, she recalled a comment that her mother had made to her, approximately three years after the event. Her mother had said, about the sexual trauma: "Yes, but you were so grown up for your age. I mean, it wasn't really all his fault, was it?"

On hearing those words from her mother when she was 14, those words that implied the abuse was her fault, Tanya had in effect been given the ultimate confirmation that this whole episode of sexual trauma had been her fault. No matter that it had occurred between the ages of nine and 12, ending with a kiss from a 55-year-old man who whispered in her ear "if you were older I would do so many more things to you". No matter at all. Because on hearing those words from her mother, it was as though she then knew in her bones that the whole episode had been 100% her fault. She had already taken on board that she was to blame for how hideous she felt about herself and that she was to blame for how ashamed she felt about the whole incident. And now that her mother had said these words, she had a fully engrained belief that she had asked for it all to happen.

When a parent qualifies our beliefs, especially our negative ones, it is like a tonne of wet cement being poured from a great height and setting quick and thick, lodging those negative self-beliefs as hard and fast as is possible, completely overriding any opposing positive beliefs that the rational brain might have been able to arrive at. This is true of both parents. But so often, it is Mum who has the greater influence, and whose wounding hurts the most.

When Tanya's own mother suggested that because she had been mature for her age that she might have had a part to play in the whole episode with the 55-year-old teacher, this tonne of wet cement poured all over her and set hard and fast. "I am bad." "I am gross." "I am dirty." "There is something fundamentally wrong with me." These were the beliefs that were cemented into Tanya's system after Mum had qualified the abuse not only as being OK, but also as being Tanya's fault. And this happened when Tanya was 14, well after those first seven, eight or nine years.

It is believed too, that the brain has another neuroplastic phase in early teens. But when we are talking about our parents qualifying our beliefs, this can happen regardless of our brain's neuroplastic stages. It can happen at any time during our childhood.

Because as we have already mentioned, our parents are like God to us. Even if we do not like our parents, even if we appear on some level to not agree with them, on a deep, core, cellular level, we absolutely take on board what they say about us as the truth. In our core, we believe them to be right. We also need them to be right – remember from Chapter 6 on shame, if our parents are wrong then we feel incredibly lost and rudderless and that is too frightening to think about. If our parents are "right", it means we are bad. And being bad is therefore the safest place to be. We make our parents right, and we make ourselves wrong. We are not capable, when we are young, with that absence of the fully developed prefrontal cortex, to do anything different.

A note to mothers

Oh mothers. What a responsibility. It's OK, we're all human, and we all mess up. As a very wise colleague of mine always says "It's not about what we do – but about what we do next". So, if there is a mother reading this, feeling hideous, please do not worry – you are not alone, and you can heal. We can all heal. One of the greatest gifts we can give our children is our healing. I am a mother too.

But we do need this level of investigation around the parent-child relationship. Because once we gain more understanding around this, it can help us to heal our wounding. And it can prevent us from unwittingly hurting our children too.

For whatever the reasons are – and we can speculate about that as much as we like – what I have come to find, doing this work, is that our relationship with our mothers seems to be deeper and more reliant on the strength of those 4 Ss than our relationship with our father. Both relationships are, of course, incredibly important in our lives, I'm not negating that for one second. But they are different. Mum and Dad do seem to have different roles when it comes to shaping a child's brain.

What about Dad?

It is thought that from conception to toddlerhood, so in those first 1000 days, that Dad's main role is to care for Mum and to be supportive enough to Mum that Mum can focus on her right-brain connection with her baby.

April came for healing at the age of 31. We worked on many past experiences around her mother, and her siblings. One day, she had landed back in time aged five years old, desperately trying to get her mum's attention. But Mum was preoccupied and this felt devastating to April. We investigated this further, and we discovered that Mum was preoccupied with Dad and Dad's needs. The five-year-old April was desperately seeking connection with her mother, but so was her dad. And her dad was winning. In this session, we dropped back in time into Dad's past. We found Dad as a small boy, also craving connection with his mother, but not able to find it. Dad's mother was preoccupied with her friends, and with the house. Dad's mother could not connect with him. April processed all of this, finding resource figures to come in and give her younger dad what he needed. She realised that he needed a hug, and that he needed to be told that he was special, and that he was loved. He was craving connection. Once this had been repaired, we brought Dad back into the scene with the younger April. No longer was he sucking the energy out of Mum. No longer was

Mum feeling torn between the needs of her daughter and her husband. April felt calm, as she witnessed both of her parents feeling as though they were enough, inside themselves. She witnessed both of her parents able to connect with her, as a child. She ran out to play, feeling joyful, free and happy.

This case study, and many like it, demonstrate the importance of our dad behaving like a grown-up in the marital relationship. They demonstrate how rupturing it can be for a child if a parent has children without having healed their own wounds. And it very clearly demonstrates one of the necessary roles of Dad in the family, which is being a support to Mum so that Mum can be fully present, emotionally, for her offspring.

It is also thought that the role of Dad comes into play much more directly with us as children, when our left brain first begins its growth, at around the age of two years old. Dad brings in a more physical and playful aspect for the toddler, who by two years old is ready to engage with Dad on that level.

And of course, should Dad engage in any behaviours that are adverse to a child, including being emotionally or physically unavailable, then this will undoubtedly impact the development of the child's brain and the child's belief systems about themselves and about the world. And we address and process all of this in the healing sessions.

But very often, it is still the relationship with our mother that will help us the most, or that will hurt us the most. And we experience that for real when we are doing the trauma work.

Where were the grown-ups?

Despite what science tells us about the importance of the connection with Mum for the child, other significant adults are also hugely important. We have already seen that Dad is also involved, and now we will look at the grown-ups as a whole, and how that can impact us too.

Anastasia, 44, feeling horribly triggered by her family life, wanted to look at why, and she wanted to heal so that she no longer felt so triggered. Her family system, as an adult, was complex with ex-husbands, ex-wives and stepchildren dynamics to navigate. Anastasia was struggling, feeling young and overwhelmed, despite being 44 years old. We went back in time, and we found the little Anastasia in the kitchen, at home, aged five, witnessing her mum and dad shouting at each other. We started the trauma processing, and Anastasia found it really hard to move through this event. She connected with the fear, the desperation, the panic, and the feelings of being lost and isolated that came with witnessing her parents fighting like children. What really worked, to nudge her system into healing mode, to really help the younger part of her to get through this and leave it in the past, was when we brought some other adults that she respected into the kitchen – in her imagination – and she was able to witness these new, wonderful, mature adults telling her parents to "grow up!". With the intervention of some emotionally whole adults into the scene, Anastasia's system was finally able to relax and let go of the helplessness that she felt around the incident of her mum and dad fighting. As a child, Anastasia had felt truly helpless, because her parents were acting like children.

So very often, when we are processing memories of our childhood, whether we are in the classroom, in the playground, or at home with family, there is a glaring absence of "grown-ups". At the time, the lack of any grown-up intervention caused this event or experience to become stuck. And very often in the healing process, in order to help the system fully process the events and leave them in the past, we have to bring in a whole new set of grown-ups to sort the mess out.

This is what our child system needs – it needs the grown-ups. The fully functioning emotionally whole grown-ups. Not the traumatised parents or the cruel, conditioned teachers, but the real grown-ups. It needed grown-ups at the time, but it didn't get them – enough. So, we bring them into the work, and the distressed child part of our system is able to finally let go and relax.

Children in therapy

If it is really difficult for a child to recover with therapy, it is very often because the parents are unwilling to engage with therapy at the same time. Many families will enter into family therapy, and this can be very helpful, but a child needs their parents to properly change at this cellular level, in order that they can fully recover; and this would entail Mum and Dad both having therapy individually so that they can work solely on themselves. All too often, the child is symptomatic (eating disorder, anxiety, depression, self-harm, suicidal ideation, messing around with drugs and / or cigarettes and / or alcohol), and the child is seen as the problem – we looked at this in Chapter 7. Yes, of course, the child needs help – that goes without saying – but so do the parents, if we want a child to recover in the quickest possible way. And in particular, we want Mum to heal, we want Mum to grow up, we want Mum to feel strong enough in her core that she can become the responsible adult in the situation. This is what a child needs more than anything: for Mum, and Dad if possible too, to do their own inner work and to do their own growing up. How do we know this? Because when we are processing those deep wounds from the past, which involve Mum and / or Dad not being available enough, all the child psyche wants in the session is for Mum and Dad to be there, as emotionally whole adults, sorting the whole situation out.

We have already looked at the notion of "intent" versus how it is received. It is really important for us to understand that just because we have a lot of trauma from our parents, it is not because our parents were bad. And if we are a parent and we haven't learned this stuff yet, *we are not bad either.*

Our parents are not "bad"

Our parents are not bad. OK, so the odd parent here and there might have been bad, sure. But on the whole, parents do the absolute best they can with the information that they have, and they honestly believe that they are doing the best for their children. It is very, very rare to come across a parent who intentionally sets out to harm their child. We might have a parent who is emotionally unavailable, cold-hearted, quick to shame, and generally pretty harsh on their children – and yes, the children will suffer residual trauma from that – but this parent is most often not intending to cause us harm.

If we think back to Chapter 4, and those diagrams that demonstrated how we, as children, try to connect with our caregivers, we can understand that our parents' less than optimum caregiving was a result of their own unresolved trauma being acted out, not necessarily their true self. This doesn't make it OK, and this doesn't minimise the impact it might have on us, but neither is it helpful to shame our parents. Parents are always doing the best they can with the information they have – and they generally consider that their choice of upbringing style for their children comes from a place of deep love. It's just not necessarily the love that our little system needs. The parent who shames their child for not doing well enough at school honestly believes that shaming will make the child do better – and thus protect the child in later life from the possible consequences of lower grades. The parent who berates their child for resting and calls them "lazy" will be worrying about teaching their child to be proactive enough to survive life. But sadly, this type of approach will in fact have a negative impact on the child's life.

All of a parent's actions come from a place of perceived parental love. But very often that parental love is informed by their own trauma, still stored deep in their system, plus the trauma of their own parents and their parents before them. Additionally, our parents' actions are informed by the thoughts and views of society at the time. And this will carry its own weight.

If all parents received the *Trauma Handbook* when they had a child, and realised how impactful their words and actions and behaviours would be on their youngsters, they would undoubtedly completely change how they react and respond to their children. But this trauma handbook does not exist for parents; therefore, as children, we are often inadvertently harmed – and, as parents, we inadvertently harm our children.

The child psyche needs more than we can really imagine. More love, more respect and more boundaries than we can probably really imagine. If we did not receive this from our own parents, we may not conceive exactly how much our own child really needs from us. The child psyche, in order that it can bloom and flourish as its own unique and powerful being, needs a parent who feels safe, seen, secure and soothed, in their core, enough of the time. Because if a parent feels this, enough of the time, then so does the child.

If a parent is not able to provide this however, because of their own unprocessed wounding, then the child psyche will be able to pick up on it.

Our healing is all about helping our younger selves to leave unresolved trauma in the past, so that we can fully grow up – at last – and lead beautiful adult lives.

Let's look at this in a bit more detail in the final chapter, on healing.

CHAPTER 10

Healing

By now we have an understanding of what unresolved trauma can look like, how we come to have it, how we – understandably – often don't realise we have it, and how this unprocessed trauma can manifest in our thoughts, behaviours and beliefs right up until we do trauma healing.

This chapter talks more about that healing. We all have some unresolved trauma. Let's now think about how we can sort it out.

Our brain is wired for love

> *"Our brain is wired for love"*
> – Dr. Caroline Leaf, Neuroscientist

Dr. Caroline Leaf, a South African neuroscientist, has spent decades researching the body, the brain and the mind. She can see, from brain scans and her work, that any adverse experience that is lodged in us – or any unresolved trauma from the past – will physically alter our brain chemistry and create toxicity in the brain, mind and the body. It is this toxicity to the brain, mind and body that makes us feel unwell physically, mentally, emotionally and spiritually. Dr. Leaf works both with people who have unresolved, emotional trauma and people who have physical brain trauma.

Of course our brains can wire in a toxic manner too – *but they do not feel comfortable doing so.* In order to maintain health and optimal functioning, our brains want to be wired for love.

Anyone who has already begun trauma therapy, or who has some experience of healing, will already understand this notion that the brain is wired for love. They will know it, because they will feel it, because they have begun the healing process. But for those of us who are a little intrepid, I wonder if it is helpful to have a neuroscientist tell us that our brains are wired for love?

All of the case studies throughout this book have used EMDR. I love EMDR, because the sessions are targeted and precise, and the results can be phenomenal. It is a very contained, directed, specific and potentially life-altering trauma therapy. And I am a big fan.

One of the things I find extraordinary about EMDR is that when we are working with past memories, no matter how horrific they might have been, as we process the dense, stuck emotion from the past, we notice that the event, or experience, or situation that we were working on no longer feels awful anymore. This is one of the beauties of EMDR. Our bodies and brains do know how to heal, if they are pointed in the right direction.

Our whole being will welcome the feeling of love that ensues from our healing.

Our brain neither welcomes, nor wants, our unresolved trauma. Our anxiety, our depression, our eating disorders, our addictions, our internal screams, our quiet apathy – they are all ways in which our brain is crying out to us for help. Our brain is wired for love, and when toxicity is present in the form of unresolved trauma, our whole being will desperately try to achieve homeostasis in an attempt to regulate itself. Sometimes we need a nudge to encourage our being to come back to that state of homeostasis and love. EMDR provides a fantastic nudge.

Remember that our brain regards unresolved trauma as toxic. Remember that our brain is wired for love. When we come to heal, we will respond willingly to this nudge.

> *The brain has an expectation of love, in the very same way that the lungs have an expectation of air.*
> – Gabor Maté

And our whole being – mental, physical, emotional and spiritual – will welcome the feeling of love that ensues as a result of our healing.

Healing our own trauma

We *can* heal from our unresolved trauma on an individual level. Our brain, mind and body will welcome our healing in ways that, in the past, we couldn't even perceive as possible. Our whole outlook on ourselves and life can change.

But healing can be messy. As Peter Levine, trauma therapist, writer, researcher and educator, so aptly states: "Trauma can be prevented more easily than it can be healed". He is so correct. Healing can feel painful and difficult. Sometimes it feels brutal too, and relentless, and sometimes it can feel never-ending. It takes a lot of courage for us to face those wounds from the past.

Healing takes time, and it takes patience. It cannot be done overnight – much as we might want it to be. It is a process, not a quick fix. But it can be done. We can heal.

Priming our internal system for healing

Gaining knowledge around trauma, as a subject, can seriously help us with the initial healing stages. We can talk about this in terms of "priming" our internal system. Many of us who have been suffering for years feel hopeless, not good enough, as though the world is an unsafe place, and we feel generally stuck in life. We do not always realise that this is because something happened to us that should not have, and that this can be healed.

We have thought for years that there is something wrong with us and that we are broken. If we had a childhood support system that did not embrace pure, unconditional love and respect, we might not even conceive that pure, unconditional love and respect is available for us. I hope that this book is helping your internal system to be primed for healing.

We can all, no matter what happened in the past, allow our brain to rewire for love. We can all heal.

Learning about our past within the framework of a trauma lens, can help particularly with us feeling seen, feeling understood and feeling validated. Learning about our story through a trauma lens also gives our left brain the opportunity to learn some information that it might not already properly know, because this information was not given to us when we were little. Our trauma will tell us that there is something wrong with us and that we are bad. And if our adverse experiences began early in life, and occurred regularly enough, then we are probably going to believe, in our core, that these messages we tell ourselves are true. To give our knowledge base a boost, to gently introduce the notion to our system that this is the trauma talking, and not the truth, learning about unresolved trauma, how it happens and how it manifests in us, is a necessary part of the healing process.

So many of us who are experiencing symptoms of trauma – from full-blown PTSD right through to being a people-pleaser, conflict-avoider, or occasional cigarette smoker – do not even realise that we are suffering with trauma symptoms and that these symptoms can be reduced with trauma therapy. Instead, we continue to suffer, whilst firmly and completely believing all of our negative belief systems to be true, and that we will suffer with the effects forever. But this is not true – this is the unresolved trauma talking.

Once we have learned about what trauma is. Once we have a better understanding of how it is has happened to us. Once we know that it is absolutely not our fault that we are suffering. Once we have taken on board all of this, then our system will feel more prepared to step forward and try some trauma work. We might not yet be fully on board though – our neural wiring is exactly that: neural wiring in the brain – and a part of us will be trying to keep us away from seeing the truth, because the truth will contradict what we are telling ourselves. This might feel weird or a bit frightening.

But perhaps we now have hope where we had none before. There is perhaps an opening in our willingness to explore. Perhaps we can see that our suffering is actually our unresolved trauma, and not the definition of the real us, in our essence. There is hopefully, now, a sense that there might exist some safety, some acknowledgement, some validation and some soothing from someone out there who not only understands our story from the past, but who actually, genuinely wants to hear it and to witness our healing with us. There is someone out there who completely understands why we feel as we do, and why we think like we do – about ourselves and about the world. And even if we still feel safer hanging on to the truth of our negative beliefs, then we at least have another person who knows these beliefs are not true and who can hold that for us whilst we journey inwards. We possibly haven't ever had that before.

A vital step in the healing process is learning about trauma and priming our system, so that we can then feel an opening to the opportunity that we too can heal.

What is trauma healing?

So what is trauma healing? Trauma healing is about identifying the blocks that are causing us suffering and preventing us from experiencing our true selves. These blocks are in the form of buried emotions and negative belief systems formed from past, unresolved experiences. They are in the form of triggers in our current lives that are affecting our ability to think straight, feel good, and enjoy a fulfilled and exciting life. Trauma healing is about properly looking at all of this, and resolving it, so that it no longer bothers us in the present or interferes with our future.

This generally means doing a little more work than just talking about our past experiences. Occasionally, talking about the past can help us to completely heal. Most often however, when we are looking at our blocks, we need to do more than just talk. Ideally we want to find a trauma therapy that offers a resolution. We want a healing modality that helps us to properly process and metabolise – in our core – any unprocessed event or experience. Talk therapy is great, and sometimes people prefer – or even need – to slowly talk before they are ready to face their innermost hurt with deep trauma therapy. But once we identify our unresolved hurt and begin to re-experience it, then a trauma therapy with a resolution is going to provide a much quicker relief from how we are feeling, than simply talking about it over and over again while feeling utterly dreadful.

For some people, trauma healing might be about living anxiety-free, or addiction-free, or rage-free, or food-obsession-free, or stress-free, or depression-free, or cigarette-free.

For others, it might look like no longer being triggered by family members, or in relationships, no longer feeling stuck in a job we don't like, or a relationship that that might be hurting us.

For others, trauma healing might look like a deep journey inwards to the soul, in order to feel a deep connection with ourselves and the world at large.

Everyone's idea of healing is different and unique to them.

What is absolutely true and consistent for everybody, however, is that we are all enough. As adults, we are all safe (most of the time), we are lovable, we are good enough, we have more control over our lives than we might think, and we have the right to feel good in our lives. And anything that happened in the past – or that did not happen – was absolutely not our fault.

You are loved just for being who you are, just for existing. You don't have to do anything to earn it. Your shortcomings, your lack of self-esteem, physical perfection, or social and economic success – none of that matters. No one can take this love away from you, and it will always be there.

– Ram Dass

And we want to heal, in order that we can embody this as our *own* truth. So many trauma survivors believe that only *other* people can feel good about themselves and their lives; but again, this is the unresolved trauma talking. Trauma healing and feeling good about ourselves and our lives can be for anyone who wants it. We do not need to carry the burden of the past through our lives.

What we can expect?

So what can we expect if we want to try some deep trauma therapy?

The six outcomes below are pretty lovely, and with diligence, very attainable.

- We will experience a massive, if not complete, reduction in intensity of difficult feelings related to past events
- Negative beliefs about ourselves will change to positive beliefs
- We will no longer feel triggered in situations that triggered us before
- When we do feel triggered, we will be able to move through it more quickly
- Past addictive behaviours will lessen, if not leave us completely
- We will want to love ourselves, and we will want to extend that love to others, from our own full cup

When we have done some serious healing, we will have desensitised painful memories from the past, we will have turned our negative belief systems into positive ones, and we will be living our life no longer triggered by people and events that used to overwhelm us. And all of this leads us towards properly loving ourselves, and others too, from a place of authenticity inside us. Research is continuing, all the time, around the brain-body connection and the adverse effects that unresolved trauma can have on our physical health. Our physical ailments can also be healed as we process our past hurts, with enough diligence and openness.

In Chapter 1, we looked at physical, sexual and emotional abuse and neglect, and the developmental deficits that ensue. With trauma therapy, we aim to heal the unresolved trauma –

the events or experiences – from this time, and we repair the developmental deficits. With trauma therapy, we will be rewiring our neural pathways so that we no longer feel the impact of the past abuse or neglect. The brain will rewire for love.

In Chapter 2, we looked at our wounding, the symptoms of unresolved trauma, and the negative self-beliefs that come with that. With trauma healing, as we process past events and experiences, our negative beliefs change into positive ones as our wounding heals. Remember, our brain is wired for love, so as we heal our wounds, our self-beliefs change too.

In Chapter 3, we looked at what happens to the metaphorical left and right brain in trauma. With trauma healing, there is a notion of us inviting our adult brain into the unresolved past event or experience, thus allowing the memory to metabolise, processing the toxicity and releasing it from our brains and bodies. And those hundreds of billions of neural pathways will all rewire to their preferred place of love.

In Chapter 4, we looked at how we shut down parts of ourselves and develop an ANP (an apparently normal part / person), building defences to keep the ANP in place and keeping all of those feelings buried. With diligent trauma healing, we can release those stuck emotions, that toxic energy stuck in the body, finally allowing those fragmented parts of ourselves to reintegrate into our being so that we feel whole. We no longer feel fragmented, and we no longer have the need to tuck emotions away, nor have defences in place to keep them there.

In Chapter 5, we looked at how we carry past trauma from our family systems, and from our parents and our grandparents. This can feel so heavy. With trauma healing, we work on our parents' trauma that is lodged in us, and the generational wounds that have been passed down to us, and we metabolise them and let them go so that we no longer have to carry them and experience them in our brains and bodies. There have also been incidents where clients have processed their trauma and noticed a difference in their parents as a result, even when their parent has not been in therapy. Quantum physics describes the phenomenon of entanglement, in which a change to a particle that has been in a relationship with another particle will have the same effect on the other particle. Therefore, if we heal our generational trauma then we will also heal it for those generations that came before us, and also for our children. We can call this the "Quantum Healing Effect", and I expect this to become very popular in the future as more and more people realise this possibility of non-linear healing.

In Chapter 6, we looked at shame and how horrifically toxic it feels inside us. As we release our shame with trauma healing, we no longer feel the need to wear a mask, or to lie, or to keep secrets. We are able to ask for help when we need it, and we become more able to trust ourselves – and to trust chosen people around us too. With enough dedicated work, our shame-based depression or anxiety can hopefully leave us too.

In Chapter 7, we looked at the family system and its relative dysfunction. The really good news is that when we enter trauma therapy, as an adult, we do not need the family system to change in order for us to heal. As we process our past material, we will find our own sense of self, separate from the family system if need be, and we will feel stronger to set appropriate boundaries with family members in a way that we never have before. We will feel empowered to conduct our lives without needing validation from our family members if our path is different to theirs.

In Chapter 8, we looked at sexual abuse. In trauma healing, we process the horror of the abuse, and all that comes with it, so that we can leave the experience in the past forever. No more flashbacks, no more panic attacks, no more nightmares, no more smell aversions, no more difficulties with sex in our adult lives.

In Chapter 9, we looked at the importance, during our childhoods, of our relationship with our parents and how devastating a rupture in the maternal bond, in particular, can be. Very often, in our trauma healing journey, this is one of the deepest and most painful and difficult wounds that we face. But we can do it. And over time, we learn how to re-mother ourselves. During trauma therapy, when we are repairing the developmental deficits, we are, in a sense, reparenting ourselves.

How long does it take to heal trauma?

This is a common question – how long will I need to do trauma therapy? I'm afraid the answer is "how long is a piece of string?".

We may now be able to estimate, having read the preceding chapters, how much unresolved trauma we have. The more we have, the more therapy it may take to heal. If we want to take a deep dive into our wounding, and we feel ready enough to do so, we might take longer. We can also dip in and out of trauma therapy if we so wish; it is intense work, and sometimes a break while we integrate our healing can be really beneficial. If our defences and safety mechanisms are deeply entrenched and we are reluctant to let them go, then it might take us a bit longer to get to the material underneath that so desperately needs the work.

Yet the timing of trauma healing isn't necessarily set in stone either. We might suddenly realise that our entire being feels different, and that our whole outlook on life has changed. And this can occur even if we are only at the start of our journey. There is no prescription for the timing of trauma healing, everyone is different.

What I can say for sure though, is that healing the "Big T" traumas – those past traumas that are more one-off events, is actually the easiest and quickest part of the process. When we are healing our developmental trauma however, it does take longer. This might feel counter-intuitive as a concept, but it is absolutely true. It is actually quicker and more straightforward to heal the event when, say, a gun was pointed in our face and we feared for our life, than it is to heal from our formative years spent with an emotionally distant or narcissistic mother.

Readiness

What I have come to discover is that healing our wounding is much more about our readiness to heal. And this readiness is not "good" or "bad". Being ready or not being ready just is. This readiness can very often equate to how safe we feel. How safe we feel in our bodies, how safe we feel in ourselves, how safe we feel in our lives, and how safe we feel sharing our stories – and our innermost angst – with those who we have chosen to help us. Some of our sense of readiness is tied in with the societal trauma that I touched on earlier in the book. If society is shaming us, we will further believe that there is something wrong with us, and we might take longer to feel ready. I hope this book will encourage your sense of readiness if you haven't felt it before.

And, of course, our defences work, as you might remember – until they don't. Readiness is very often linked in with how well our defences continue to work, or not. If they cease to work for us, we might want to look at the trauma underneath and heal it; it might be ready to be looked at by this stage. Even with our defences still firmly in place, if we have a desire for them to leave us then we can start trauma healing. Because this desire is part of our readiness.

Safety and self-protection

Our adaptations to trauma – our defences – act as self-protective measures. These self-protective measures serve to keep us feeling a sense of safety. It might be a false safety, but it feels safe to us. We might experience addiction to substances or people, or overworking, people-pleasing, overscheduling, seeking relationships. We might have an obsession with making money, numbing with food, starving ourselves or over-exercising. We might be behaving narcissistically, or simply have feelings of disconnection from others. Or perhaps we struggle with a sense of self. The list goes on. All of these maladaptive behaviours –

these external vices – are giving us a sense of safety that we are not able to feel deep inside ourselves. But they can also hurt us.

One of the first steps to healing, therefore, is to find a sense of safety that does not hurt us. This might be through a trusted friend, or a practitioner with whom we feel good and in whom we can trust. It might be a yoga teacher, a therapist, a meditation coach, a dance teacher, or a 12-step fellowship group. We will all have our preferred space where we can tune in and know, somewhere, on a cellular level, that a part of us at least feels safer in this space than we did before.

There are yet even more people who believe that they find their joy in external pursuits. We are all looking to enhance our lives, and many of us find this enhancement through drinking, drugging, overeating, over-sexing and so on, without realising that actually we are numbing ourselves. Numbing is not joyful at all. Numbing is a state that we put ourselves in, with the help of a substance or behaviour, that actually takes us away from our inner state of feeling fully joyful and alive, *in the present moment*. We are probably using external substances and behaviours to find a sense of joy, because our unresolved trauma is inhibiting any deeper sense of joy that is inside of us already. Or perhaps we have been incorrectly taught from our childhood – and from life – that external "things" are a main criterion for bringing us joy and happiness.

These numbing behaviours will bring to us a sense of safety; a sense of safety that we have not been able, before now, to fully realise inside ourselves.

We do not need to feel 100% safe in order to start trauma

healing – we just need to feel safe enough to start. Our feelings of safety will increase the more inner work that we do, and the more we feel safe around the person with whom we are doing the work.

And then the healing journey can begin. It might be crazy fast, it might take years. It doesn't matter. It is not a race. But if we want to heal, there are ways that we can do it. We can heal.

I am such a believer in healing. I am truly converted. I used to be a very traumatised individual, dissociated, numb, acting out on anything external I could get my hands on, believing I was born wrong, unlovable, not good enough, and that I was permanently damaged.

I can honestly say that, as a general rule, I don't experience that any longer.

I truly believe that every human being has an innate ability to heal. If we want to.

However, because we have not been raised in way that celebrates or embraces healing, we can massively benefit from a nudge in the right direction to get our system into healing mode, or at least further towards being ready to start. And if we didn't receive those 4 Ss, or we have some big, unresolved traumas, then trauma therapy with a trusted therapist can be incredibly beneficial.

Putting the work in

The healing journey is not necessarily easy or straightforward. It is not like taking a pill. It is a process, and we have to properly be a part of that process. What this means is that as and when we are ready, we face and release deep pain and previously engrained emotions and belief systems that have been buried inside us for a long, long time. When we do this, we turn them all around, and we think well and feel good as a result.

We do need to put in the time and the work though, we really do. And it is hard work.

All of the pain we have stored in our bodies hurts like hell. And our self-protective layers, however maladaptive and dysfunctional they might seem, are helpful to us because they help us to feel safe. Safe from feeling the pain, safe from feeling rejection, safe from feeling abandonment, safe from feeling not good enough. They also serve to soothe us – to soothe the child part of us that didn't feel safe enough to be ourselves, or the child part of us who wasn't co-regulated enough and soothed enough when we were young and in distress. These protective layers are keeping us safe and soothed so that we can function – they are literally allowing us to live our lives.

These behaviours and belief systems might appear dysfunctional and maladaptive, but by goodness do they have a loving purpose – a benevolent intent. They are protecting us from our hurt. They are super loving – and they are on our side, believe it or not! And it is helpful for us to realise this. We are not acting out on our unresolved trauma because we are "bad", we are doing it because our system feels unseen, unsafe and unsoothed on the inside, and these behaviours are helping us to feel seen, safe and soothed. These behaviours are helping us to regulate ourselves.

Very often, the idea that we might heal, and subsequently have to let go of these maladaptive behaviours and belief systems, can feel quite frightening.

So we start our healing journey from exactly where we are. There is no right or wrong. Our body will tell us what is ready to be healed – and what is not yet ready to be healed.

Many of us don't even know that healing might be possible, because we have become so accustomed to our dysfunctional behaviours that they are our normal. And even when we realise that we want to change, and to heal, it can still feel scary.

Healing does seem to be a layered process. Rather like an onion. You can't peel deeper layers of an onion until the outer layers have been taken off. The same is true for trauma healing. And every trauma healing modality I have ever worked with completely respects this layering. How can it not? We will only come forward for, and respond to, healing when we feel ready and safe enough to do so.

Willingness

Sometimes, what we need more than anything is a willingness – a willingness to start. If our adaptations and self-protective measures are very strong, and we are very reluctant to put them down, and we are consequently too "walled up" to look at what might be underneath because it feels too far away or too frightening, then just having the willingness is a start. Just having the willingness that, at some stage, we might not want to have food ruling our lives, alcohol ruling our lives, cigarettes, shopping, workaholism, people-pleasing, dysfunctional relationships, apathy, always saying 'yes' when we want to say 'no', or excess fear or feelings of shame ruling our lives. Just having the willingness to want to change can be enough to start.

Releasing our victimhood

When we carry unresolved trauma from the past, we are still carrying the energy of a victim. This is because, of course, we have been a victim. We have been a victim of less-than-optimal events and experiences. We are a victim of trauma. And until we heal our wounds, we will continue to carry the victim imprint with us. When we continue to carry feelings of victim however, we feel stuck. We cannot move forward. We continue to run into situations that fit with our victim status, and we find we connect more with other people who are victims too. We feel overwhelmed and alone, and sad. And this does not serve us.

When we heal, we no longer feel like a victim. Once we have circled through, addressed, felt, experienced, faced and fully processed all of the emotions around what happened to us in the past, we release our victim status. Once we have properly addressed all of those past experiences, we can feel compassion. We have compassion towards those who hurt us, and compassion for all of those who have not yet found their own healing. And we find compassion for ourselves. This compassion can move us through victimhood and into our power, as we realise that we are no longer just surviving, but that we are thriving. We are thriving with a deep sense of compassion for both ourselves, for others, and for the world in which we live.

Discovering compassion

Our brains are wired for love, remember. Not just love for ourselves either; this also encompasses our capacity to love others – to love everything. When we heal, we love each other again, and we support each other, regardless of age, race, religion, colour, or gender. And because we now know, on a deep level, that on the inside we are enough, we also feel as though we have enough on the outside too – regardless of how much material "stuff" we may or may not have. And we can see that everyone else is exactly enough too, regardless of how they might be acting out on their pain. We feel compassion for our fellow humans, in our core. And we can live our beautiful lives in our wholeness.

Finding compassion for those who hurt us

As we heal, we discover feelings of compassion. But what about those who hurt us? Can we find compassion for these people too? Initially this might feel like an impossible concept, but we can do it. Actually, we *need* to do this.

Our ultimate healing position is to have genuine compassion for our abusers. And this is truly possible, regardless of whether we have been physically, sexually, or emotionally abused.

We can pause during the work, and we can take a break – of course we can. But if we stop doing the work before we have reached a place of compassion for those who abused us, we might continue to feel like a victim, and we will feel like a trauma survivor. If we continue, however, until every last shred of difficulty has been processed, and we can accept what happened and feel compassion towards those who abused us, then we will have become a trauma thriver.

As we feel compassion for those who hurt us, our hearts will swell, and we will be able to feel love for them all. We won't love their behaviour, oh no, their behaviour was unacceptable and what they did should never, ever have happened. But when we have fully confronted the pain around what happened and completely processed it, then we can separate out the hideous behaviour of our abusers, and we can feel compassion for the traumatised humans that they were. When we do this, we can live much more from a place of open-heartedness, in all areas of our lives. And we can live from a place of radical acceptance.

Radical acceptance

In order that we can leave our victimhood in the past, arrive at a place of true compassion and properly thrive, we want to have a feeling of radical acceptance around the past. We cannot change what happened back then, whether it was Big T trauma or developmental trauma that shaped us. But we can face those past hurts, those past events and experiences. We can face them head-on, and we can process them.

As we do this, as we process through all of the layers of difficult emotion that have become lodged inside us: the terror, the panic, the shame, the disgust, the anxiety, the fear, or the grief, they properly leave our system. Once they are completely gone, then we can start to release our victimhood in the story, and we can embrace a radical acceptance of what happened, with compassion, and without any difficult or painful emotional charge remaining in our bodies.

Healing and the bigger picture

When I look at the world and humankind through a trauma lens, in the same way as I have attempted to put across in this book, I see suffering as a result of unresolved trauma everywhere. It is evident on an individual level, and also on a societal and collective level. I hope you can now see this too.

Our unresolved trauma makes us feel disconnected; disconnected from ourselves and disconnected from others. Our unresolved trauma drives the notion of "separate". When we feel disconnected and separate, we will do almost anything to make ourselves feel connected and safe. But, as we have discussed, we will choose superficial ways to achieve this. To find our sense of safety, and a sense of belonging, we often strive for "more" external measures – more food, money, alcohol, people, distractions, relationships, things. We seek more and more of these, as we gain a sense of safety from these acquisitions and hobbies, hoping that our sense of safety will increase at the rate of our acquisitions. Yet our yearning for more creates more separateness, and our separateness drives us even further away from others – and further away from our core selves too.

Our need for external safety measures, and the separateness that inevitably comes with it, creates a type of selfishness, a self-centredness, as we strive to overrun others in order to get what we think we need (think panic loo roll buying at the start of the Covid pandemic, for example). Yet we don't feel more connected or safe just because we have a bigger home or more parties – or an extra stash of toilet paper. We think we do, because we think these things bring a sense of safety to our disconnected being. But these things can all be taken away. And once they have been taken away, we are back to feeling unsafe and disconnected inside once more.

Healing is where we find real connection, and real safety, inside ourselves. When we heal, we can start to rate our individual needs at an equal value to those of our fellow humans. When we feel a sense of healing, we strive to help others, rather than surviving solely for ourselves.

With healing, we can live from a place of love for all beings. We can end our separateness and live from a place of compassion for all. And when we can do this, we can enter the cosmic dance of the universe where we are all connected, all one, and all loving.

The future

The generations of children that are being born now have more awareness than ever before. They are more evolved than ever before. They are born understanding most of what is in this book already, from their inner knowing – as a part of us did too. But we need to honour this and show our children that what they know instinctively is actually true. We are their role models while they are young, and we now understand the importance – the criticality – of raising all children with the unconditional love and respect that they deserve.

A future that works better for all humans and the planet needs a loving perspective. But our unresolved emotional pain is driving our need for more. We live on a planet that will simply not be able to sustain our demands if we continue to take from it in the way that we have been doing. If we remain in our traumatised separateness, if we remain stuck in our unresolved pasts, then we simply will not have a planet to live on anymore.

It might all feel like a monumental task when looked at like this. And it is. But monumental does not mean impossible. Monumental just means that we need to make a start. Now. And we can start by healing ourselves.

Nobody is broken. We all have some trauma. And trauma can be healed.

Acknowledgements

In writing this book, I have been inspired, guided and supported by so many colleagues, clients and friends whom it's difficult to thank adequately.

Starting with the bigger picture, this book would not exist without the pioneering work of Bessel van der Kolk, to whom I extend the deepest gratitude for placing trauma, and trauma treatment, firmly onto the clinical map. In addition to Bessel, other enormous contributors to the field of healing trauma, my understanding of trauma, and this book include Peter Levine, Gabor Maté, Ana Isabel, Jim Knipe, Donald O. Hebb, Dan Siegel, Allan Schore, Alice Miller and Dr. Caroline Leaf, all of whom I have quoted or referred to directly in the text. Other great professionals whose work I refer to indirectly include Carl Jung, Gregory Bateson, Rachel Yehuda, Thomas Hübl and Stephen Porges. Thank you all.

In the ever-expanding field of EMDR practice, I extend my thanks to those who have trained me personally in this incredible therapeutic method. Laurel Parnell, Mark Brayne, Robert Lefever, Matt Wesson, Barbara Lerch and Jim Knipe in particular.

I would like to extend my deep gratitude to The Recovery Centre, Knightsbridge, for the continued support that I receive from you. I love you all. Thank you.

Enormous thanks to Carl White. Thank you for your wonderful editing, encouragement and whole-hearted support. You also taught me that sentences of 83 words or more can be really quite challenging for the reader. You have helped me to make this book possible in so many ways. What a blessing you have been. Thank you.

Thank you to the team at SpiffingCovers. James Willis, thank you for understanding the book from the moment I described it to you. Thank you to Stefan, for designing such a wonderful cover. And to the team of editors at SpiffingCovers, thank you for all of your dedicated work.

A particular and warm salute also to my clients. Without your courage and dedication, for your showing up and embarking on this deep, inner work of healing, this book would never have happened. I thank you from the bottom of my heart. Not only have you made this book come alive, but your stories will inspire readers to embark on this type of deep, therapeutic work themselves. Thank you.

Finally - centrally - thank you to my children.

I used to hear the phrase "your children are your greatest healers" and I did not fully understand what it meant. But I do now. My children reflect back to me those parts of my psyche that need healing. They do not (yet) know they are doing this, nor as children should they. We've hopefully learned from this book how important it is for children to hold all the rights to their own childhoods without feeling responsible for their parents. But if we as adults can take on board what our children are showing us when we feel triggered, that we are the ones who need healing not them, then this is such a gift.

Acknowledgements

In no small measure, it's the light that my children shine on my dark places that draws me into the inner work, and to the growth that comes from going deep. I do this in equal measure because I want to be the best version of myself for them. They deserve nothing less. One day, kids, you'll be ready to read what your mum has sought to put down in words here. I hope you'll be able to appreciate how grateful I am. I just hope it didn't show too much.

About The Author

Lucinda Gordon Lennox, MSc, MBACP (Accred), is a psychotherapist specialising in trauma. She works as a consultant at The Recovery Centre, Knightsbridge, and also has a private practice.

She has trained in EMDR with Matt Wesson (EMDR Academy), Laurel Parnell (Attachment-Focussed EMDR), Mark Brayne (EMDR Focus), Jim Knipe (EMDR Toolbox) and Barbara Lerch (EMDR Centre London), and is a member of the EMDR Association UK and the Parnell Institute in California. She holds a master's (MSc) in Addiction Psychology from London South Bank University and is an accredited member of the British Association for Counselling and Psychotherapy (MBACP – Accred).

Living in London and working internationally online as well as in-person, Lucinda writes for UK media outlets on wellness and mental health, and for the Elephant Journal in the US, lecturing also on the impact of trauma on family systems as part of the MBA programme at the Instituto de Estudios Superiores de la Empresa (IESE).

As a mother of two and with her own experience of recovery and family, Lucinda is passionate about emotional wellbeing, and in particular the transformative power of EMDR to heal the impact on both society as well as individuals of trauma-driven wounds of the past.

Printed in Great Britain
by Amazon